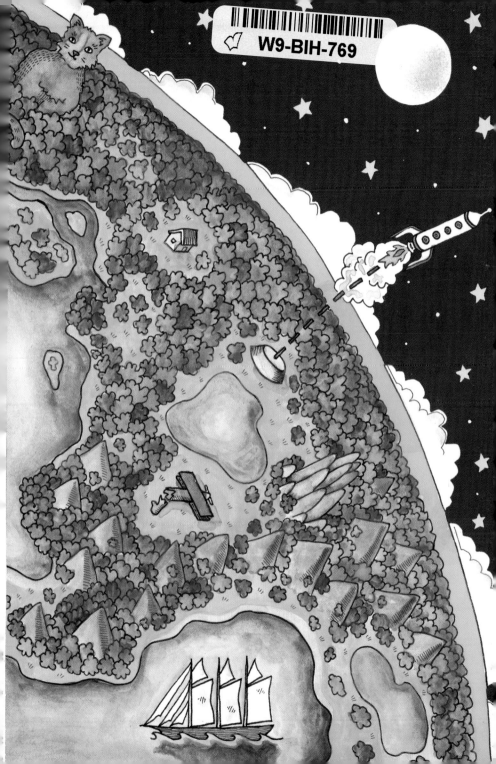

www.826chi.org

IBSN: 978-1-934750-50-6

Book design by Alison Kuczwara

Book Illustration by Marnie Galloway

Big Shoulders logo design by Robert Soltys

Printed in USA

BIG SHOULDERS
BOOKS

www.bigshouldersbooks.com

$\overline{THE}\,826\underline{CHI}$
COMPENDIUM
——— *Volume IV* ———

An Assemblage of Writings by the Students of 826CHI

———

Chicago, Illinois
United States of America

———

Foreword by Christine Sneed

CONTENTS

LEGEND

WORKSHOPS	FIELD TRIPS	AFTER SCHOOL TUTORING & WRITING	IN-SCHOOLS	PARTNERSHIPS

SECTION II: ABROAD

SECTION III: PAST

SECTION IV: FUTURE

SECTION V: WITHIN YOUR CITY

SECTION VI: WITHIN YOURSELF

FOREWORD

Christine Sneed

This tidy but mighty little book that you're peering down at right now might not look anything like a giraffe's long ladder of a neck, or a swirly rainbow lollipop, or a glow-in-the-dark soccer ball, but it has something in common with all these remarkable things: it's perfect!

Behold its firm, finite dimensions, its sleek and slippery cover that opens and closes with a modest whap! You can see quite well where it begins and ends, but what's inside patiently awaits your gaze (and your super-powered, listening ear). At the moment, this book is docile as a sleeping dog, and it's up to you to wake these words up.

Wait...while I have you here, let's leap to another metaphor or two (it's good to stay limber, don't you think? As long as you don't stretch too far and split your pants, which, um, might or might not have happened the other day to someone I...er, well, we'll leave it at that.) Like a magician's satin, crow-black cape of myriad secret pockets, or the handheld tunnel of a kaleidoscope spun to make its vibrant, shifting picture-puzzles, I can tell you that from here on in wonders are in store.

The young writers whose stories and poems you'll find in this paper-and-ink magician's cape have minds filled with marvelous places, people, and things, with Martians and grand-motherly dinosaurs, with UFOs and jungle birds and underwater science labs. There's no shortage of rockets or marshmallows or moons either.

You'll also find an alien from the Planet of the Apes who is transformed by an enterprising scientist into Lady Gaga, and you'll meet a number of very hungry zombies in a Choose-Your-Own-Adventure story.

Still not convinced you're in for a thrill ride better than any hours spent sitting before that glowering box in the living room? You know the one I mean—the squaroid object that gapes blankly all day at the windows or at that portrait of you dressed up like a banana last year for Halloween when no one's home to push its buttons. Yes, that's the one—the brooding box you and your folks might bicker over when you want to watch American Idol or Dancing with the Stars but your mom DVR'd Sunday's 60 Minutes and also insists that you watch last Tuesday's program on PBS about pine trees—the one you wouldn't wish on your worst enemy!

Right here you have the answer to all your problems—this spiffy new book. Oh yes, turn off those Simpsons reruns and get ready to travel to London and Afghanistan, to Mars and back, to a secret cave in a tropical rainforest. No jetlag or vaccinations to worry about, no power cords, plane tickets, batteries, or satellite dishes either.

Just in case you're still not convinced that you should dive in with both eyes and both feet, I've prepared a list of twelve good reasons (one for each month of the year, for each astrological sign, for every egg in the carton) to get ready to witness squishy but courageous jelly beans fight evil robot pelicans, and Michael Jordan save the world from a mythical laguar (a superfast creature that's a cross between a lion and a jaguar) bent on burning up all the world's most beautiful cities.

Okay, here we go:

1. There are no scary dentists in these pages, no dental appointments or even a lengthy rendezvous with your toothbrush.

2. There are, however, plenty of marshmallows, Oreos, fudge, and a big jar of Nutella. You'll also find bacon, tortillas, hamburgers, and a mysterious foodstuff called a cheeserock.

3. Justin Bieber makes one or two special guest appearances. Yes, the Justin Bieber.

4. A tough older brother is nice to his younger brother.

5. Boys and girls fall in love and survive to tell you about it.

6. All plane crashes contained herein are only simulations.

7. When the world is falling apart, Walgreens is still open.

8. Not only will you read about pelican robots, you'll also meet a Spanish gorilla robot named Niko!

9. You'll learn some important facts. Here's an example: in the fifth century B.C., Chicago's name was Dumboland.

10. This book contains one of the most inventive rhymes known to humankind: Pistachio Mustachio.

11. These writers have seen the future, and reassuringly, it still contains dogs and dogwalkers.

12. This book never needs to be recharged.

So now, without any more shoulder-shrugging or pillow-fighting or gum-popping, please tie your shoes, zip up your coats, pat down that last unruly curl—things are about to get wild and imaginative.

...

    ...

        ...

           ...

                ...

                    ...

P.S. Wait a second...did you hear that? No? Well, maybe I'm just hearing things. No, hold on...I heard it again. That's laughter—great, big booming laughs coming from the pages you're about to start turning. Uh oh. I hear a sob or two too. Yes, I confess, there are some tears in here to go with the joy, but you know how it goes—you need the dark to make the light that much brighter.

P.P.S. Yes, those are indeed leaves on the trees just outside your door, not small green vampire-like bats sent from outer space.

port of call

— *Section I* —

SPACE

Demise of the Robot Pelicans

⭐

by Audrey Pettigrew, Grade 6

FROM

Gather 'Round with Groupon!, Spring 2012

"5, 4, 3, 2, 1..."

The scientist screamed the numbers. And then his plane crashed.

Dr. Waffenschmidt blinked and rubbed his eyes; he had left his contacts in again. But then he realized he wasn't sleeping—he had been knocked out.

"My plane!" Dr. Waffenschmidt yelled, sitting up abruptly.

Dr. Waffenschmidt found himself in a valley, with pieces of his plane strewn everywhere. He began to look around and take in his surroundings. The valley was broad and surrounded by tall cliffs and colorful rivers. But despite the beautiful surroundings, there were no people. And so Dr. Waffenschmidt began to wander.

Following one of the colorful rivers, the doctor walked up a steep incline, huffing and puffing. By the time he got to the top, he was exhausted. He stopped to take a breath and noticed that nearby there were many little huts that looked like doghouses. Curious, Dr. Waffenschmidt tip-toed up to the nearest hut and put one eye up to the window.

Inside, the doctor saw a bunch of things that looked like large jelly beans. Squinting, he was surprised to see mustaches on their bodies. Suddenly, one of them moved, and the doctor jumped in surprise. They were living creatures—a whole family of them.

Inching toward the door, the doctor tried to get a closer look, when one of the jelly beans noticed him. Squeaking squishily, all of the jelly beans jumped and ran to hide behind their sofa.

"No, don't be scared!" Dr. Waffenschmidt cried. "I only need help for my plane that has crashed here!"

One of the jelly beans slowly crept out from behind the couch and approached the doctor. As he moved, he made a soft, squishing noise.

"You're not a pelican!" the jelly bean exclaimed in a British accent.

"Why would I be a pelican? I'm a scientist—Dr. Waffenschmidt, to be exact!"

"A scientist! Maybe you could help us. My name is Hubert, and I always wanted to be a scientist—until the evil pelicans destroyed our science academy."

"Well...maybe I can help you. But a favor for a favor—only if you help me to fix my plane."

"Of course!" Hubert exclaimed in an overly excited voice.

Together, Hubert and Dr. Waffenschmidt began to plan how

to defeat the evil pelicans that were plaguing the town. But they did not realize the danger to come.

From above, the flock of robot pelicans spied the plane pieces scattered around Squishy Town. Rumors were growing that a new sort of creature had arrived.

Of all the pelicans, only Pelican Bob was smart. The others were simple creatures, their only duty, the only thing they were programmed to do, was to destroy jelly beans.

"We must find who this new creature is and destroy it!" Pelican Bob commanded the other pelicans.

They all agreed in unison, making a horrible gurgling noise, like the sound of jelly beans rolling around in metal stomachs. They began to fly toward the jelly bean village.

Back at the village, Hubert and Dr. Waffenschmidt had decided they would re-program the pelicans. No longer would the birds terrorize the jelly bean town.

"So instead of eating you, they will eat the grass that grows all over Squishy Town," Dr. Waffenschmidt explained.

"That's brilliant! I see why you're a scientist; you have many brilliant ideas."

"Thank you, Hubert. But it will be difficult. How will we capture these creatures?"

"I have an idea," Hubert replied sadly.

"What is it?"

"I could be bait. The pelicans will surely come flying at me. I'll jump onto one of their backs as fast as I can and then open them up to cut the necessary wires to re-program them."

Hubert's jelly bean wife emerged from the hut and began to protest. But Hubert calmed her down and convinced her that this was the only way.

In the distance came the disgusting gurgling noise. Hubert, his wife, and Dr. Waffenschmidt looked up at the sky in terror. But Hubert was ready to put his plan into action.

Hubert hurried his wife back into the hut and ran to the edge of the hill the village sat on top of. Dr. Waffenschmidt shouted encouragements at Hubert and handed him the supplies necessary to do the job: wire-cutters, a hammer, a screwdriver, some nails, and a Q-tip.

They saw the pelicans flying closer, with Pelican Bob at the head of the flock. Behind Bob was a smaller pelican.

"I'm going to try that smaller pelican over there!" shouted Hubert. "He will be easier to get on top of!"

The pelicans started swooping down toward the village, destroying huts and grabbing screaming jelly beans. Hubert ran toward the small pelican, jumped on his back, opened his head with the hammer, and re-programmed his wires with his tools.

Now acting much less aggressively, the first pelican flew down toward the ground and began to eat the grass.

"It's working!" called Dr. Waffenschmidt, hiding from the pelicans behind a bush.

Confident, Herbert jumped from the small pelican's back to

a larger pelican, and then another, and then another, re-programming the birds as he went along. Eventually, it seemed as if all had been re-programmed, with the birds now all eating grass.

Hubert, having done his duty in saving the beans, jumped onto the ground and cried out, "Dr. Waffenschmidt!"

Hubert and Dr. Waffenschmidt came together on the field. Tears formed in Hubert's little jelly eyes as he saw the destroyed huts and dead jelly beans scattered everywhere.

"You don't have to help me anymore," Dr. Waffenschmidt said. "I'll stay here and help you rebuild."

Suddenly, a large pelican rose up over the crest of the hill, directly behind Hubert. Hubert turned, but not in time—the pelican pecked him with his giant metal beak. Stunned and injured, Hubert managed to get on top of the pelican, and with his last breath broke open the pelican's head and rearranged his wires.

The pelican became docile, Hubert fell to the ground with no squishy breaths left.

A few days later, the town's survivors decided to throw a party to celebrate the pelican's defeat, but their hearts weren't in it. Everything was different because so many jelly beans had died.

From the side of the party, a pair of glowing red eyes watched the jelly beans. They were pelican eyes, belonging to a pelican not eating any grass, but flying in the darkness. It was Pelican Bob—waiting and plotting his revenge.

G-Rex Versus the Bacon Invaders

by The Students in Mrs. Lowe's 4th Grade Class

FROM

Nettlehorst Elementary School, Spring 2013

Once upon a time, there was Grandma T-Rex who had a purple mohawk and wore red glasses and a green dress. She really liked to eat bacon, her nails were painted pink, and she lived in a sewer on Mars. She also carried a purse that she could use as a weapon. In her home in the sewer, everything was decorated pink with doilies. She always had tea at three o'clock in the afternoon.

One day, she was knitting. She enjoyed knitting golf club covers and socks. Her husband, Grandpa T-Rex, was gone for the day. Her friend, an alligator, came over for tea. His name was Jerry, and he had red hair. They enjoyed some sugar cookies, scones, and sewer water with their tea.

"This is the best meal I've ever had," said Jerry.

Grandma T-Rex replied, "In my day, tea was never this good."

Jerry, who was a plumber, often wondered, "What would happen if bacon aliens invaded Mars?"

Grandma would always respond, "Oh, I'm sure that would never happen."

Grandpa T-Rex was swimming that afternoon, which is what he did every afternoon. He would swim for hours, all the way out to visit the tar pits.

Grandma and Jerry were drinking their tea when they heard an ominous sizzling sound. They looked in the closet, but there was nothing weird in it, just a chainsaw, more green dresses, and knitted leg warmers. The sizzling grew louder. They looked in the oven and only found a coconut cake. At that moment, Grandpa T-Rex burst into the house and shouted, "Take cover, the Bacon Invaders are here!"

The Bacon Invaders were giant strips of bacon with faces and pointy teeth. They were holding guns full of orange juice. The leader of the Bacon Invaders was a talking sunnyside up egg named Yolky. They were after Grandma T-Rex and Grandpa T-Rex because a long time ago, Yolky and the Bacon Invaders had tried to take over Mars. They failed because Grandma had fought them off with her purse. This time, however, the Bacon Invaders and Yolky had brought escargot, which is French for snails. The escargot were snails from France and were there because the T-Rexes had eaten their grandparents.

Yolky and the bacon had traveled into the sewer on a waffle boat. Grandma and Grandpa T-Rex had gone to shut all the openings but not before the escargot had thrown butter and garlic bombs into the house.

"It's time for revenge!" declared Yolky. One of the Escargot banged down the door and said, "Au revoir, Grandma!"

Space Invaders and Newcomers: Don't Attack Earth!

by Ingrid Gonzalez, Grade 5

FROM

A Bubble With a Password, Fall 2012

My important message to the Martians will be, "NEVER attack Earth, because it's beautiful!" The first reason you aliens should not attack Earth is because it's the only planet we can live on. We rest and we go to class on Earth. You might be wondering, "What are these human things?" To go to sleep, you go on a soft marsh-mallow and lay down and close your eyes. You go to sleep at night when the bright sun goes down.

When the sun goes back up, you go to school. School is where they give you work that you have to do at home. At school we learn interesting, new things every day, like social studies, reading, and math. Like I said, they give you work that you have to do at home. This is called homework. I don't know why they give out homework, maybe to go to 826. 826 is where they help you with your homework.

We also have cars that are kind of like your UFOs, but different. I can see that your planet is boiling hot. Does your spaceship have a way to cool off? Our cars have a machine that throws cold air in our faces!

There are so many more things to learn and see that I really want to tell you about, but you might get really scared. And that's why you shouldn't attack Earth! If you do attack, don't complain when we come to your planet. Don't think we can't come, because we'll bring our space suits. One other thing: You really need air conditioners. If you don't want the air conditioners, then give them back so we can get a refund.

The Sonic Cosmic Cow Force

by *Students in Mrs. Brescia's 5th Grade Class*
—— FROM ——
St. Helen School, Spring 2012

In the year 4012, there were flying cars and flying cows with metal wings and lasers in their eyes. Protecting the Earth, Moon, and the entire galaxy was the Sonic Cosmic Cow Force (SCCF). The members of this superhero team were Nicky, Briana, Chris, and Leslie. Nicky had super sonic speed. Briana had invisibility powers. Chris had telekinesis powers. And Leslie had super strength.

One day, aliens crash-landed on the Earth. These aliens were fat, round, and green. They had antennas and used a lot of bright red lipstick. They seemed really friendly because they brought so many yummy-looking cupcakes for everyone on the Earth. These cupcakes had rainbow frosting, and the cake part was swirly, half chocolate and half vanilla.

But the frosting had sleeping potion in it that would make

everyone fall asleep. The aliens planned on making everyone on Earth fall asleep so they could steal rocket ships (because they had crashed their own ships) to head up to the Moon. They really wanted to eat the Moon because it tasted like mozzarella cheese, and they could not get this kind of cheese on their own planet.

This was a serious problem, because over one million people lived on the Moon, and it was where the SCCF liked to hang out.

The aliens started passing out their rainbow frosting cupcakes on the Earth, and since they looked so good, everyone ate them and fell asleep.

Meanwhile, the SCCF were hanging out on the Moon. They noticed something fishy was going on down on Earth because they saw, through their telescope, the rockets getting set up for launch and that everyone was asleep.

"Hey, check this out," said Chris. "Isn't it weird that everyone is asleep but the rockets are being set up?"

"It must be the aliens from the crash earlier," said Leslie.

So the SCCF headed down to Earth, and the aliens tried to give them cupcakes.

"Try our delicious cupcakes! We just made them today, and we want everyone to have a free sample," said the aliens.

Yet, Nicky noticed that everyone who was asleep had rainbow frosting on their face.

"Hey guys, this is not a good idea," Nicky said.

"I agree," Briana said. "Look! They're getting away!"

The aliens hopped on the Earth's rocket ships to go to the

Moon, but Briana turned invisible and followed the aliens into one of the ships.

On the ship, Bri heard the aliens talking: "Our plan is working! The cheese will be ours!"

So, Briana used her invisible phone to alert the SCCF of the aliens' plans.

Nicky grabbed Chris and Leslie and sprinted super, super, super fast to a rocket ship to chase after the aliens.

On the ship, Chris had an idea. He used his telekinesis to move the Moon back and forth so the aliens could not land, giving the SCCF enough time to get to the Moon and stop the aliens.

Meanwhile, Briana snuck into the engine room of the aliens' ship and pulled wires to make the engine stop. The ship continued toward the Moon, but it only drifted slowly. This delay gave the rest of SCCF more time.

On the SCCF's rocket, Leslie came up with an idea. "Hey guys, what if we put pepper and hot sauce on the Moon? Then it would be too spicy for the aliens to eat."

"Yeah!" Nicky and Chris said, while exchanging a high-five.

So, Nicky, Leslie, and Chris found a huge pepper shaker and a humongous bottle of hot sauce. The hot sauce was extremely hot, the kind that makes you cry. Leslie used her super strength to carry the shaker and bottle and sprinkle it all over the Moon before the aliens could get there.

Finally, when the aliens arrived, Briana jumped off the ship and joined the rest of the SCCF. Everyone smiled and said,

"Welcome to our Moon! Have a bite!"

But when the aliens started eating the Moon, they started to cry. The mozzarella cheese was so spicy, and they HATED spicy food.

"You can have your Moon back," the aliens cried. They went away to a new galaxy and never came back again.

The people on the Earth woke up once the sleeping potion wore off. The SCCF continued to keep the Earth, the Moon, and the galaxy safe.

The End

The Cool Machine

*by **Aileen Vasquez, Grade 2***

FROM

Our Next Destination is Outer Space, Spring 2012

One day, I found a pair of 3D glasses. I put them on and went to the park. There, I saw a gigantic machine. It was grey and tall, like a skyscraper. The machine had rockets, and on the front of it was a giant clock. There was a seven-foot-long window that you could look out of.

When I put the 3D glasses on, everybody looked like green aliens. The aliens had antennae in order to smell food, like pizza. The antennae were creepy, because they had little polka dots on them. When I took the glasses off, everyone looked normal. The machine took off when I got on it. The machine took me to outer space. I saw Pluto, the smallest planet. It looked like a face hanging on a string.

Creating Spacecrafts

by **Noah Boehm, Grade 6**

FROM

A Bubble With a Password, Fall 2012

If I was president and an alien invasion was coming, I would tell the citizens of the United States that the U.S. had found an alien spacecraft and had manufactured copies of the spacecraft. We were going to have a test in 10 days, and all citizens should not panic if they see any U.F.O.s, but they should get to a strong building in case of any malfunctions. I would not tell the people all of the facts, so the citizens would not riot or panic and destroy cities, government property, or anything else in the U.S. This would be like politics today, not giving all the facts and lying about the important stuff.

Section II

ABROAD

Caught in a Bad Romance

by Students in Mr. Nix's 3rd Grade Class
FROM
UNO-Marquez Charter School, Winter 2012

Once upon a time, there was a superhero named Charles Gaga the Giant. He was born on the Planet of the Apes, and he could grow to a huge size and read minds. Charles also had four eyes, blue hair, green skin, and a dollar sign tattooed on his chest. This was as close as he could get to looking human. Now that he was on Earth, he wore his disguise to blend in. The reason he wanted to blend in on Earth is because the food on Earth was far better than the food on his home planet. His favorite food, flying centipedes, had all flown away from the Planet of the Apes when everyone started to eat them to extinction. On Earth, though, Charles Gaga could use his tongue to capture his meals. He settled down in the Amazon forest and ate bugs all day.

Charles Gaga was being watched, though. There was a scientist named Doctor Alex who lived in a telescope in the middle of the ocean (just under Jamaica). He was very tall and chubby, and he always wore his evil goggles and a hamburger shirt. Dr. Alex noticed something strange on his Alie-O-Meter.

"Hmm, looks like we have a situation," Dr. Alex said. The Alie-O-Meter was mooing and quacking! Dr. Alex said, "That must mean there's an alien nearby." Dr. Alex had spent his entire life trying to prove that aliens existed, and now was his chance. He decided to fly his pet polka-dot beluga whale to the Amazon rainforest to pursue the source of the mooing on the Alie-O-Meter.

Charles Gaga was in the middle of eating a centipede when he heard the unmistakable sound of a polka-dot beluga whale in the distance. It sounded like a rooster and a monkey combined. "Cocka-Eeee-eee-eee!" it said. Charles Gaga knew he was in trouble. The polka-dot beluga whale was the loudest animal in the universe and would scare away all his food. Charles Gaga knew he had to stop the whale before his meal ran away.

Little did he know that Dr. Alex was riding on top of this particular whale. Charles decided to use his super growing powers and face off against the whale. He grew larger than the Willis Tower and tried to swallow the polka-dot beluga whale in one gulp. But Dr. Alex was sneaky and captured Charles Gaga in a cardboard box he had designed to control aliens. It was labeled, "May Contain Aliens."

"Hooray, I've captured an alien. It's hamburger time!" Dr. Alex said. Dr. Alex took Charles Gaga to his secret Jamaican lair, where he strapped him into his Huma-tizer machine. When he turned the machine on, Charles Gaga shrunk to human size and became

Lady Gaga.

Dr. Alex broke down crying and asked for her hand in marriage. Lady Gaga just danced. The two former enemies became husband and wife.

Even though Charles was now Lady Gaga, she never lost her taste for flying centipedes. Together, they lived happily ever after on their centipede farm.

The End

The Magical Adventure: In the Land of Cheeserocks

A Choose-Your-Own-Adventure Story

by **The Students**

IN

826CHI's Elementary School Writing Camp, Summer 2013

One day, Uncle Bubba was in the bathroom. His bathroom had a fridge and he was very bored, so he started eating a piece of magical cheese. He felt like he wanted to jump out of a window. Suddenly, he jumped out of the window, and he jumped so high that he ended up in the Land of Cheeserocks. In the Land of Cheeserocks, there were many dead birds and hills made of rocks that you could eat (because they're made of cheese). These rocks had cow faces on them and were poisonous to birds. When Uncle Bubba arrived, he felt sleepy because the pressure was so high. Uncle Bubba met a stranger named Mr. Frank, who only wore black. Mr. Frank invited Uncle Bubba to his house.

If Uncle Bubba went to Mr. Frank's house, turn to **page 76**

If Mr. Frank asked Uncle Bubba to give him the magical cheese, turn to **page 109**

The Defense of Scar

by **Micah Kohng, Grade 3**

FROM

Villains Reclaimed!, Summer 2013

I am Scar from the Lion King. Everyone hates me because they think I took Mufasa by the paws and threw him into the stampede. Well, that wasn't me. It was another lion. He had different colored fur! I was on the plains, hunting. I took a nap, and I woke up when some random gazelle called in my ear, "Mufasa is dead!"

I'm the brother of the king, so I had to take over as king. I had no choice! Suddenly, Simba appeared out of nowhere and challenged me. He eventually threw me into the flames. I survived, but they kicked me out. Tell Simba to look at the evidence. It wasn't me!

The Bear and a Tiger and a Snake and a Dragon

by Julian Ventura, Grade 1

FROM

A Bubble With a Password, Fall 2012

Once there was a bear. The bear attacked a tiger in the rainforest. A snake jumped on the tiger and the bear. Then the tiger and the bear went into a dragon's cave. The dragon burned fire at the bear and the tiger and the snake. And all of them started running to a lion, and the lion said, "If you still fight, I will call your mom."

The Fifty-Foot Kitten

by Carlos Jimenez, Grade 3

FROM

Our Next Destination is Outer Space, Spring 2012

I was in the jungle and discovered a new animal. It was a fifty-foot kitten, and it ate and ate and ate and ate dogs. When he finished the last dog, he started eating Xbox 360s. I had no choice but to make a thirty-foot yarn ball and roll it deep into the jungle. The kitten chased it into the jungle, but he will be back!

Saving Rainbow London

by *Students in Mr. Bernier's 7th and 8th Grade Class*

FROM

UNO Esmeralda Santiago Charter Elementary School, Spring 2012

In a faraway place called London, there lived a soldier named Frank. Frank had green eyes and brown hair and wore rainbow-colored camouflage. He also carried a book bag. Inside that book bag he had all of his supplies, including mayonnaise, bread, a slingshot, and a paper gun.

It was early in the morning when Frank walked down the street. A rainbow-colored movie store stood in front on him. Frank sighed and said out loud to himself, "I'm nervous and tired," and walked into the store. In the back of the store there was a magic portal. Frank did the Hokey-Pokey, and the portal opened up. The magical store had the magical supplies he needed.

On the counter was a talking cash register named Sir Moneybags, who asked him: "What do you want? You can only pick three things in this magic store."

Frank replied, "I need a magic coin, a bracelet to make me invisible, and a magic net."

"Fine, you can take these things if you tell me I'm the best cash register in the world," Sir Moneybags murmured.

Frank sighed, "You are the best," and grabbed his things and tried to walk out.

"You forgot something, Frank," said the cash register.

"Thank you," Frank replied and walked away.

Frank made his way over to Big Ben carrying his supplies. Across the street there was a monster playing Frank's video games. Frank got mad and walked up to the monster. The monster was huge and black and white, with big teeth and red eyes.

The monster said to Frank, "I want the world to be black and white, and I will be the ruler." The monster sprayed black and white paint from his mouth over everything around him.

Frank got mad and said, "Oh no he didn't!" He attacked the monster with the bread and mayonnaise. The monster liked the food and started to eat it instead of hate it. Frank thought his plan was ruined.

Frank took the rest of his food and put the magic coin on top of the pile of the food. The monster went to eat it and was distracted by the coin. While he was bent over eating and looking at the magic coin, Frank threw the net overtop of the monster, trapping him in its magical net powers forever.

The powers of the magical net brought the monster back to his senses. "The world is supposed to be full of colors, not black and white. I will repaint a rainbow on everything you ruined," Frank exclaimed.

"You're right soldier; colors are beautiful," said the monster. As he realized this, the monster's black and white colors faded, and he turned into a brilliant rainbow of colors, too.

Frank felt bad for the monster and decided to keep him as a pet. He walked back down the street with his new pet, and they played video games all day, eating bread and mayonnaise sandwiches.

Untitled

by Stefania Betti, Grade 6

FROM

Alexander Graham Bell Elementary School, Spring 2013

It was 1990 in Afghanistan, Shali was resting on the toshak on the hard cement floor of her family's apartment. The door flew open. Shali immediately covered her face and hunched over, worried it would be the Taliban. Relief flooded her when she heard a soft, childish voice say "Hey! Wanna hear what happened today, Shali?"

Shali revealed her face and turned towards her eight-year-old brother, Ari. Shali was now angry. If a Taliban was there instead of her brother, a twelve-year-old girl would be shown no mercy.

"Don't ever do that again! I thought you were the Taliban! You scared me half to death!" Shali yelled at Ari. She did this rarely. He was her only brother and would be her only friend.

Ari tried to do a puppy dog face, but Shali wasn't buying his terrible acting.

"Whatever," Ari said, obviously giving up. "I saw the most bizarre thing today!" he exclaimed, his eyes lighting up.

Shali tried to hide her excitement and eagerness. "What happened?" Shali asked.

"Well, it all started with a small protest in the market, but more and more people started coming, and eventually it turned into a huge riot! The Taliban were beating them with sticks and the butts of their gun, but the protesters used their bare hands. Eventually they either escaped or got arrested. It was so cool!"

Shali had her mouth hanging open with awe, but she quickly realized and shut it closed, making a smack sound with her teeth hitting each other.

Ari continued smiling.

"What's wrong with you?" Shali asked.

"I have a present! I found it at the market; no one was selling it, so I got it for free." Ari pulled out a red balloon from behind his back.

"Wow!" Shali was amazed—so much excitement in one day!

Ari and Shali went outside to a small courtyard and played with the balloon until the sun disappeared. Shali was so tired that when she tried to grip the balloon it slipped out of her hands and floated up in the night.

Ten years later

Ari was on the run. The Taliban was after him because of a riot. Red flames were everywhere, sparks in the air, blinding everyone. Ari stood up on a bench and waved the flaring red sparks into the night sky. Shouting was everywhere, but Ari just chuckled. He ran before the Taliban could see him, but he was already found, known, wanted.

Ari was in a building. Someone slammed open a door. He held his breath and closed his eyes. A man with big, cold hands gripped his neck and dragged him outside. He knew right then it was over. Afghanistan was in trouble, and so was he.

To Be Continued

The Magical Adventure: In the Land of Cheeserocks

A Choose-Your-Own-Adventure Story

Continued from page 109

If he bent the cheese and found out that it was fake cheese with broccoli inside...

After Uncle Bubba got the fake cheese from Mr. Frank, he tried to bend it. It broke open, and there was broccoli inside. Uncle Bubba ate the broccoli because he thought that it was blue cheese. The broccoli transported him to Broccoli World, with tall tree stalks made of broccoli and an evil broccoli king named King Broccoli.

However, King Broccoli hadn't always been called King Broccoli. He was born as King Stega. When he was little, his parents wouldn't let him have any precious broccoli. When he was older, he tried it for the first time and he loved it. So he changed his name, and started to pillage the country for broccoli. He used broccoli to make a castle and a potion that takes you to Candy World. Uncle Bubba saved a broccoli tree, and King Broccoli rewarded Uncle Bubba with the potion.

Uncle Bubba drank the potion, and was transported to Candy World. There, Uncle Bubba ate a lollipop, not knowing that it was actually another special potion that would take him back to the real world. When Uncle Bubba arrived in the real world, he had the lollipop in his hand. The lollipop was infinite - whenever it was finished, it would come back. Uncle Bubba saw his best friend Henry Crary and said, "Ha ha ha! I got an infinite lollipop!"

Henry Crary said, "Oh no! Can I get some?"

Uncle Bubba said, "No."

That night, Henry Crary snuck into Uncle Bubba's house and stole the lollipop. He took it home and finished it. He threw it away because he didn't know that it was infinite.

Uncle Bubba woke up, crying, and knew who did it because he saw evidence from a hidden video camera. Uncle Bubba walked to Henry Crary's house and got his lollipop back.

Henry Crary's wife divorced him because he cried too much about losing the lollipop.

The End

The Puffball

by Leenish'a Pettigrew, Grade 6

FROM

They Want to Kiss The Sidewalk, Fall 2011

There is a type of bird named the puffball. It has an upside-down face, and when you look at it, it looks back at you with confusion. The puffball is about three feet long. It only eats fish, and it finds food by going to lakes and hunting. No other animal eats puffballs because they throw off bacteria to kill the animal that's trying to hunt them. They really don't have to do anything to avoid being eaten.

The puffball lives in trees in the rain forest. It has camouflage wings, and it communicates by making "ka, ka" sounds with its beak. The puffball is special because it can transform itself into any animal or any object. It can change itself into any object such as a sock, or any person, like Justin Beiber.

The puffball dies once every five weeks. Then it comes back to life after it rebuilds its stamina. After that, it comes back as a baby, but with very big eyes and different colored wings. Puffballs only have brightly colored wings when they are young. When they get older they lose their color and become camouflage.

Once, a puffball flew to Brazil and visited Rio. He found a ton of birds to chillax with. But one day, the puffball and his friends were watching T.V., and they found out that Justin Bieber had cheated on Selena Gomez. They found a map that led to Justin Bieber, and when they finally found him, they shipped him to 826. Then 826 shipped him to Admiral Moody. Then things happened. Some ugly things.

The Importance of People in a Plane Crash

by Eric Saucedo, Grade 4

FROM

An Elevator with Different Floors, Winter 2013

Usually Kate and Patrick stay at home and play video games and stuff, but today they are flying to Hawaii. They both get on the plane. Patrick is going to fly the plane because he's a pilot. Kate goes to the eightieth seat because she doesn't want to sit by Patrick. She doesn't like sitting by nerds, and Patrick is a nerd.

Right when they are halfway there, the plane says, "WARNING! Something is wrong!" One of the engines breaks. Then they find an island, and they land. Well, they crash land.

They carefully and quickly climb out, and Patrick tells Kate to gather tools and anything she can find that will help to rebuild the airplane. They find coconuts to eat, branches for ladder transportation, animal manure for fuel, and they train cheetahs to become maintenance laborers because cheetahs work fast. Patrick knows if they don't go at least fifty miles per hour they will stay stuck in the tree. They put the cheetah laborers on treadmills in front of meat to get more engine power. It works!

They blast off out of the tree, but thirty minutes later they fly into a thunderstorm and get scared. Patrick loses control and falls out of his chair. Then the meat falls, distracting the cheetahs, and they crash. But this time they don't survive, not even the cheetah laborers.

The Inventions of Ashley and Niko the Spanish Gorilla Robot

by **Students in Mrs. Lowe's 3rd Grade Class**
FROM
Woodson South Elementary School, Winter 2012

Once, there was a Spanish gorilla robot named Niko who could jump really high and loved to dance and eat bananas. He had red eyes, very sharp teeth, and a big nose. Niko lived in a secret underground lair deep in the rainforest. To get there he had to crawl underneath a tree stump and into a tunnel.

Niko was an inventor, which is why he had a laboratory in his secret underground lair. In his laboratory, he was working on two wonderful inventions. One was a hybrid banana, which gave everyone who ate it the ability to run super fast. He was also working on building a time machine. He was helped in building these inventions by his trusty friend, a toucan named Ashley.

Ashley was very helpful because she could fly around the rainforest and collect the materials Niko needed for his inventions.

One day, while Niko and Ashley were busy working on their new invention, Niko said, "Ashley, I need some more bananas for working on my new hybrid banana and fueling the banana-powered time machine. Can you please go find me some?"

"Awesome," said Ashley. "I will go get some and come right back."

Ashley climbed out of the underground lair and began flying through the rainforest, looking for bananas.

The time machine Niko was working on was very colorful and had lots of buttons. It also had a seat like a rollercoaster. The time machine was nearly ready, but the problem with using it was getting enough bananas to power the machine. It took three hundred of them!

Meanwhile, the evil chameleon, Dr. Brain, who had spectacles and a mustache, was constantly disguising himself as other people. Dr. Brain was also trying to steal Niko's time machine. He knew about the time machine because he had been spying on Niko and Ashley by changing colors to blend into the environment.

Little did Ashley know, as she flew around the rainforest collecting bananas, that Dr. Brain was about to interfere with her plans. All of a sudden, Dr. Brain jumped out from behind a bush and trapped Ashley in a cage.

"Get me out of here!" Ashley yelled. "What did I do to you?"

Harnessing the Nacleopoluo

by **Michael Noonan, Grade 6**

FROM

Our Next Destination is Outer Space, Spring 2012

Day 23:

(Morning)

I am currently in a tropical rainforest in a cave. I was driven to this cave by a new animal species called Nacleopoluo. The Nacleopoluo has the features of a frog, but it has poisonous venom that it injects like a sleeping powder into your skin. They dwell at night and find food by making their prey fall asleep, and when another carnivore kills it, the Nacleopoluo eats the remainder of it.

The Nacleopoluo is the size of a cat and quite aggressive. When in combat with another species, they spit at each other. Their spit has sleeping powers, and since it goes through the skin, the winner is always the one that is not sleeping on the floor. The Nacleopoluo has a few predators because they can occasionally become drowsy. If I could only harness the...

Alexander III, Dr. Platypus, and the Perfect Pumpkin Battle

by *The Students from Mr. Zielinski's 4th, 5th, and 6th Grade Class*

FROM

Drummond Thomas Montessori School, Fall 2011

High above the floor of an abandoned apartment building, on the top of a bookcase, was Slug City. Prince of the Slugs, secret spy Alexander III, reigned over his slugs wearing a red velvet cloak that could barely contain his huge muscles. His biceps were bigger than his brains (he had two brains). Alexander III was also bald and always wore his Super Droopy Spy Goggles because he was blind without them.

Down at the tip of the peninsula where the apartment building stood was the entrance to Alexander III's arch enemy's lair. What looked like an average chimney was the tube that traveled twenty million leagues down to the underwater fortress of Dr. Platypus and his army of dopey, mutated dragonflies.

Dr. Platypus and Alexander III had been enemies for thirty million years, even though both their mothers had told them to stop fighting twenty million years ago. Their argument had started over one perfect pumpkin. Both slug and platypus wanted it, but in the end Dr. Platypus managed to steal it from the patch first. Little did he know, the pumpkin was poisoned, and when he ate the seeds his IQ dropped immediately by five thousand points. Bitter because he could no longer be a doctor, he vowed to take his revenge on Alexander III. "You'll rue this day, slug!" yelled Dr. Platypus before he descended to his underwater lair.

With his assistant, Queen Elizabeth IIVXMLX, the retired evil twin of a well-known ruler, Dr. Platypus created an army of killer dragonflies and Pistachio Mustachio, a delicious and evilly fake soda devised to end Alexander III once and for all.

"Lizzy, go deliver this bottle of Pistachio Mustachio to that slimy, idiotic slug. I will finally have my revenge for that pumpkin!" ordered Dr. Platypus.

Queen Elizabeth traveled all those leagues and all those miles to the abandoned apartment building, set the soda down, rang the doorbell, and dove back into the sea. SPLASH!

Hearing the doorbell, Alexander III went to investigate. As soon as he set his Super Droopy Spy Goggle eyes on the bottle of Pistachio Mustachio, he saw the sparkly 568 mustache molecules intended to destroy him.

"Nice try, Dr. Fartapus. He thought the 568 mustache molecules would harm me, but with my special slug DNA, it's only going to make me stronger," rasped Alexander III. He chugged the soda in five seconds and immediately grew a long, luxurious rainbow mustache. The bottle of Pistachio Mustachio also made him able to fly. He grew wings and, using the mustache to steer as he glided, Alexander III flew to the Land of Blue Nail Polish to train with the Master Slug. After three hard weeks of training, Alexander III was ready to face Dr. Platypus.

He went to the Land of Butterscotch where he knew Dr. Platypus would be. (He was in a butterscotch field.) While he was flying over looking for his enemy, Alexander spotted the Perfect Pumpkin!

"The Perfect Pumpkin is mine," he shouted in mid-air. But as he dove towards it, Dr. Platypus came out of the trees and started running toward the pumpkin. As slug and platypus both reached for the pumpkin, a black hole appeared out of nowhere, and the Perfect Pumpkin disappeared forever into the unknown.

"This is all your fault!" they both shouted at once. Dr. Platypus called his dragonfly minions. A battle raged for one minute and then abruptly ended when Alexander III ate Dr. Platypus. And so his enemy lived eternally and internally in his stomach.

"Mmmmm, that needed ketchup," laughed Alexander III.

— *Section III* —

PAST

When I Met My Soulmate

by **Malik Jones, Grade 11**

FROM

Catching Feelings, Winter 2012

When I first saw this girl, I said to myself "she is going to be the one who gets me stuck." Her name was Aaliya Armstrong. She was a light-skinned girl who was about five feet, four inches. As she walked past me, I wanted to talk to her, but I was very shy. I turned around to get my Cheetos from the stand, and I went to the counter to pay for them.

As she walked behind me, I started to get very nervous. I thought to myself that I can do this and gargled up enough guts to talk to this girl. I walked out of the store, hoping she wouldn't reject me. She finally walked out of the store, and I asked her name. She told me. I asked if I could walk with her, and she said, "Sure." As I walked with her back to her home, I asked questions like how old she was, and she was the same age as me.

I asked her if she had a boyfriend, and she told me no. I asked her what happened, and she said that she had been single for three months. She went in the house and came back out of the house just for me. That moment showed me that if she was my girl, she would do anything for me. She made me happy at that moment. I went in for the kill and asked her, "Could I be the other half of your heart?"

Every time I saw her from that moment on, she made me happy. When I called her, she would always say, "I was thinking about you," and it made me fall deeper in love. I was love blind, like she was the only person I saw. She would always give me a kiss when I saw her and left her. Love is still a priority with her, going on two years.

I remember the first time she kissed me on my front porch. When she kissed me, I felt like I was flying in the sky. Her lips felt smooth and soft, like a honey bun with icing. She was the one I wanted to marry if I ever got married. She stole a piece of my heart and locked it in her heart to keep a piece of me inside her.

She sent me through the tunnel of love, which made me catch feelings. When she kissed me, I thought she was the only girl on earth. Aaliyah was the one that I wanted to love all my life. For minutes while her lips were pressed on mine, I could feel nothing but joy and happiness. I loved a lot of girls before, but I have never felt enthusiastic and continuous love like this girl has made me feel.

Continuous love made me feel great. I'm in the sky from her

kiss. It was exciting, and I never wanted to leave her. If I could stay with her every day, I would live with her. The way she has me, I don't think another man has felt this way. Her lips softly move away from mine, and my feelings stay. Complete silence— no cars passing—just us as we pull away from each other and stare at each other.

Santa Goes to Jail

*by **Richard Gomez, Grade 1***

FROM

They Want to Kiss The Sidewalk, Fall 2011

Santa went to jail and he yelled at the police.

Eplaca Girl

*by **Saffiyuh Ouyoun**, Grade 4*

FROM

Elementary School Writing Camp, Summer 2012

My name is Arina, but I'll tell you a secret. I'm actually a superhero. I'll tell you how it started. Before I was born, my mother's first husband died in the military. My mother still had high hopes, though, so she decided to go to space. When she was on the Lost Planet, where nobody had ever been before, she found green slime everywhere. She put on her blue lab gloves and picked up the slime. She carried a barrel full of slime back to her science lab inside of her rocket ship. While she was examining the barrel of slime using a microscope, there was a slurp and a hiss. All of the slime turned into a person! My mother let out a high scream.

The man said, "Don't worry, I won't harm you." She immediately calmed down. Days passed, and the two became good friends. Sadly, my mother had to leave the Lost Planet. The Slime-Man wanted to stay in touch. He put a microchip into her shoulder and told her, "It will keep you protected and give you superpowers. If you ever need me, you can push on your shoulder and I will come right away."

My mother went back to Earth. She got married to another man named Brandon, who was also a scientist. He had brown eyes and black hair. A month passed, and my mother got pregnant. She was working in her lab until three hours before I was born! She rushed to the hospital, and her husband held her hand and said, "Calm down, I'm right here."

Then I was born. I have brown eyes, just like my father, and superpowers, just like my mother. I can lift things up by focusing really hard on them. If I want to hide, I throw an egg at the ground and disappear into a thick cloud of smoke. When I was one year old, my mother noticed that I could lift my bottle from across the room. When I turned four, my parents were so impressed with my powers that they bought me a purple cat named Skingy, who smells like roses. Skingy scares off the evil animals of the villains I fight and protects me.

My neighbor's name is Marlen. We have been playing together since kindergarten. Sometimes, when we were in his backyard, I would see him point at something, and it would lift up. When he noticed I had seen him, he would drop whatever he had lifted.

"You didn't see me make that watering can fly, did you?" he would ask.

I said no for a long time, until we were seventeen and I decided to tell him about my superpowers. Now, Marlen is my sidekick. His super mouse can transform into any animal!

Marlen's mouse and Skingy the cat came to college with us in Texas. Before we left, my mother got sick. Just before Marlen and I were going to graduate, I heard the news: she had died. She didn't die because she was sick, though. She was killed by the evil Ivy Man and his sidekick, Leopard Skin Girl. Now, it's up to me and Marlen to get revenge.

To Be Continued

Mike Fink Between Volcanoes

by **Jackie Acosta, grade 5**

——————— FROM ———————

Neighborhood Bridges, Fall 2011

There was once a man named Mike Fink who was hiding from Annie Christmas, the world's strongest lady. He had told her, "Hey, you! How about you cook me up some food!" He got so scared that he ran all the way to Texas. But Annie found him.

"Hey, you, five-foot Mike Fink, I'm going to teach you a lesson for what you said," she told him.

"AHHHHH!!" yelled Mike Fink.

Annie pushed him so hard that he landed between two volcanoes that were about to erupt. When a boulder was headed his way, Allle flew down on her jet and picked him up. "I wouldn't really hurt you," she said. "But I wanted to teach you a lesson."

The End

The Magical Adventure: In the Land of Cheeserocks

A Choose-Your-Own-Adventure Story

Continued from page 41

If Uncle Bubba went to Mr. Frank's house...

Mr. Frank's house was a creepy old shack, and there were 54 zombies living in the basement. While Uncle Bubba walked down the cheese stairs to the basement, he got super scared, grabbed a leaf blower, and blew it into the zombies' faces. The wind was so strong, it blew some of the skin off the zombies' faces.

Mr. Frank yelled at Uncle Bubba, "Please stop doing that! You're being mean to the zombies! I'm in love with one of them! Her name is Zombea."

"What do you mean you're in love with that zombie? They're trying to kill me!"

"They're not mean zombies, they're nice zombies!"

Meanwhile, the zombies laid a trap on the stairs for Uncle Bubba. The zombies didn't know that Mr. Frank was going up the stairs first. Mr. Frank got caught in the trap, which was a big, unbreakable, plexiglass box.

Zombea got mad at the zombies that set the trap and kicked them down the stairs. After she kicked them, she tried to set Mr. Frank free from the trap, because she secretly had a magic wand that none of the others knew about. But she didn't know that the trap had a keyhole, and magic didn't work. She needed a key and a magic recipe, which the zombies were hiding in a secret place in the basement.

Mr. Frank, who couldn't hear what was happening outside the trap, kept cheering because he didn't know Zombea didn't have the key. Zombea started crying, and disintegrated.

*If Uncle Bubba tried to free Mr. Frank by looking for the key and the magic recipe, turn to **page 182.***

*If Uncle Bubba tried to escape the creepy old house by going through the Zombies' obstacle course to the exit, turn to **page 184.***

Annie Christmas
Above the Trees

by **Cheyenna Thomas**, *grade 5*

FROM

Neighborhood Bridges, Fall 2011

Once there was a lady, Her name was Annie Christmas, Annie Christmas was so tall that when she entered a room she had to duck down. She was strong and could pick up a car. She wore a glittery Christmas dress all year long.

One day there was a man walking past a tree and he heard somebody say, "Help me." He thought the tree was talking and he was scared.

He yelled, "Who's there?"

"Me," whispered a voice from the top of the tree. The man looked up and saw the glittery dress and knew it was Annie Christmas. "Oh," he said.

"Help me down, please!" Anne screamed in a panicky voice.

"No, you wouldn't make me food when I asked you to three years ago."

Annie remembered that he hadn't asked nicely. Then she said, "When I get down, you're gonna wish you'd helped me!" Then Annie remembered she had a rope. She used the rope to take her water horse. Annie tied the rope to the branches and climbed down the tree. The man ran away as fast as the wind. She caught him with her rope and put him on top of the tree. Now if you go to the forest you have hear him saying, "Help me." He sounds tired.

The End

A Boost of Adrenaline

*by **Daniel Dardon, Grade 6***

FROM

Poetry Bump!, Summer 2013

The janitor tripped over a bush that was in the
middle of the river.
This bush was not an ordinary one.
You know how a rose bush is prickly.
This bush's pricks were pocket knives.
As you can probably picture, it was very bloody.
Also, since he was in a river, the water turned tremendously red.
He was losing blood by the millisecond.
While the river was gaining it.
Thankfully, I was there to relieve him of
his torture and save him.
I felt a boost of adrenaline.
I felt crazy.
I flew a jet.

It's Not The Size of The Man in Love, It's The Size of The Love in The Man

by **Residents of Mercy Home for Boys & Girls**

FROM

Summer 2012

Once upon a time, in fifth century B.C., in Dumboland (which would someday become Chicago), on Jackson Street, there was a juke joint called Twerk Academy. This night was unlike most nights at Twerk Academy, because this was the annual Halloween Juke Jam, where guests had to find their matching mask partner. King Little Caesar, the most bossy and miniature king in the land, arrived at the Juke Jam on his horse named Ferrari. The king laid his eyes on the biggest queen in the nation, who was so beautiful he felt like he was a broke man seeing money.

"O day, o day. What is this I see? But a beautiful, happy queen!"

said King Little Caesar. The queen's name was Queen Big Sally, but she was known to everyone else as Bill. She was six feet tall, with long, blonde hair that reached the bottom of her strong, big, sweaty back. She was so strong that she could lift two horses and walk at the same time.

"Oh King, I love your horse," she said while she eyed his horse with hungry eyes. She knew that she must have the horse to eat, because that was the only thing that could satisfy her hunger.

The king knew that he would never be happy unless he was with her. So he set out into the Dark Forest to hunt every rare bald flying bear with lazy eyes. He knew that would impress her. Bald flying bears with lazy eyes were attracted to stinky breath because of their love for garbage. So the king went into the middle of the forest and let out the biggest, stinkiest yawn because he had the stinkiest breath in the world. His stinky breath was a mixture of mildew and burritos.

Out of the Lost Trees came the bald flying bears with lazy eyes. The bears came kicking through the air. As the bears neared, the king pulled out his clean tranquilizer full of Lysol, since the bears were allergic to cleanliness, and shot the bears square in the forehead.

The happy king dragged the bears with his rope back to town, excited to impress the queen. As soon as he saw the queen, he became so excited that his little feet slipped out of the stirrups, and he fell to the ground.

Having never seen the king standing before, she had never

realized just how short he was. But she became mesmerized by the delicious bald flying bears with lazy eyes. So, the king's height did not matter to her because she knew he would always be able to care for her and feed her bald flying bears.

And the king hunted and the queen ate happily ever after...

The Magical Adventure: In the Land of Cheeserocks

A Choose-Your-Own-Adventure Story

Continued from page 185

If Uncle Bubba believed the zombie, who was telling the truth, and goes to find the bell knowing that it will make the zombies fall asleep and he can escape back into Cheeserocks...

Then Uncle Bubba traveled home and found a good job as a shipper. He bought a house in Holeston Park.

Uncle Bubba was very lonely. He had no wife, no family, and no pet. So he met a girl and asked her on a date.

Ending by Zayd Puzon, Grade 3

The Outing

by *Kaprisha Martin, Grade 11*
————— FROM —————
Catching Feelings, Winter 2012

The sun blazed as my mom and I walked over to the car. I opened the door and slid into my seat. I smiled and bounced in my seat while my mom started the car. It felt like a lifetime had passed since I saw her last. I couldn't wait to spend some quality time with her. We were going grocery shopping, but before that we had to run a few errands.

"Hurry and turn on the radio, crazy lady!" she yelled as the engine revved.

She tore down the street, only slowing for stop signs. I turned on B96, our favorite station, just as they started playing "Firework" by Katy Perry. My mom and I looked at each other. Then, rolling down both our windows, we screamed the lyrics at the top of our lungs. Other cars on the street looked toward us with weird faces. We just laughed and drove on. Three songs later, we cruised to the corner of Washington and parked. I got out and followed her into a barber shop. She waited for a big man dressed like a woman to notice her.

"Eylonn!" he screeched and ran to hug her.

"Cleo!"

They both seemed so happy. I felt myself kind of fall into a dark corner in my mind. I was pulled back by Cleo.

"And how's my godchild?" he asked.

"Oh I'm fine. Good," I murmured.

"My goodness, you're so big. Still look just like your mother."

I smiled shyly and wiggled my fingers around.

"That's my pride and joy there, Cleo. Straight A's across the board." My mom beamed. They began to start their conversation, and I went to sit down. I felt the darkness creeping again. I was jealous. I didn't mean to be, but I was. This was supposed to be my time with her. I didn't know how much time passed, but my mom shook my shoulder out of nowhere.

"Come on baby, it's time to go," she cooed. I said our goodbyes and walked to the car. She pulled on my arm softly to stop me.

"I'm sorry about that." She smiled with her lips turned down. "Maybe we should go shopping for earrings."

I smiled back at her. I missed her so much.

"Yeah, we can do that," I said. We walked to the car and drove off, music blasting.

Mysterious Mittens

by Abigail Czajka, Grade 8

——— FROM ———

One is Bald and the Other One Isn't

Once upon a time, in a land far away, there was a pair of...
MITTENS! But these weren't any ordinary mittens; these mittens
didn't need any hands to move. Everybody in town had heard the
story of these mysterious mittens, but they never believed the
tales. The only person to ever actually see the mittens was Bob,
the grave digger. But Bob was now old and never left his home for
anything but trips to the market. And ever since he told his story,
whispers about Bob flooded the town. To this day, if you ask Bob
about the mysterious mittens, he'll tell you the story.

The year was 1960. He had just finished work and was about
to leave. He got in his car and started on his way home. He was
speeding up, when... he slammed down on the brakes! As he looked
out of his windshield, he could not believe his eyes! There they
were—the mittens—just as everyone said. But just as fast as they
appeared, they vanished! He was anxious to tell everyone about

his discovery.

The next morning, he threw on the first clothes he could find and ran outside, into the town square. As he ran, although everyone stared at him, he didn't realize that the clothes he had picked up were old and very dirty! Even if he had known, he wouldn't have cared, because he was far too excited. He came to a halt in front of his buddy, John.

He yelled, "John you...you ha-"

"Woah, woah, woah! Slow down there, you've been running!" John said, cutting off Bob.

"I know! Just listen! I saw them!" Bob said.

"Hold on, saw what?" asked John.

"The mittens!" Bob shouted.

"Oh, my goodness! Are you serious? You know that's just a story; those things aren't real," John replied.

"No, really. They were red, and wool, and they had a set of little bionic legs, six of 'em!" Bob yelled.

"Please, you're just saying that! No one's ever seen them, and nobody ever will! You know why? Because they don't exist!" John said.

"You'll see! Just 'cause you don't believe me doesn't mean I'm lying! I'll tell everyone in town. They're smart enough to believe the truth!"

Bob ran up to the podium in the center of town and called everyone over. Yelling into the microphone, he said, "Here! Over there! Everybody, listen! Come on over!" The townspeople looked around, confused, but at the same time, very intrigued. They walked over and surrounded Bob. He repeated his story to the crowd, and as he did, they whispered into their neighbors' ears and expressed their disbelief. The crowd looked up at the podium and booed at Bob until he strolled off the stage.

Bob began to walk home, but while Bob walked on, somebody from the crowd shouted in his direction, "No! Stop, I've seen them too!" Bob turned around and looked at the man, and Bob knew he was right!

The Life of My Father

by **Sebastian Guerrero, Grade 6**

——————————— FROM ———————————

They Want To Kiss the Sidewalk

A long time ago, my father would walk to school. After school, he would go to work. He cleaned houses for people. He had to work because he was poor. He had eight brothers and three sisters. Every day, he and his family ate only beans, rice, and tortillas. My dad only had two cars as toys. His family had only one house phone. My dad made the most money of anyone in his family. For fun, they swam in natural spa waters or the lake. And now he has become the manager at his window washing company, and sometimes I help him with his work.

The Mystical Laguar

by **The Students in Ms. Woodruff's 5th Grade Class**

FROM

Rowe Elementary School, Fall 2012

Once upon a time, there was an animal so fierce and fast that no other could even dream of catching up. It was called a laguar. It was a mixture of half lion, half jaguar. But this story is not about any ordinary laguar; it's about the very first laguar: Steve Rumplestiltskin Cookoo.

Steve had the body of a lion, and the color of a jaguar: jet black. He had one yellow lightning bolt stripe along his back, and he was so fast that, when he jumped, he practically flew.

Steve was invented by Dr. Fringell, the maddest and most evil scientist in the entire dimension, because the doctor needed help taking over the whole world. Dr. Fringell lived in the jungle and was Albert Einstein's evil brother, so they looked identical.

His original plan was to have Steve destroy the universe with his laser eyes.

So, right when Steve was born, the doctor said, "Steve! I want you to go to the following places: New York, Rome, Chicago, Las

Vegas, and Rowe Elementary School. When you get to these places, I want you to destroy EVERYTHING EXCEPT CHILDREN! They are precious, and we need them for our plan as mutated minions."

"Yes, master," replied Steve, and he ran/flew away.

Steve decided to travel to Rome first. On his way, he saw the Colosseum, the Leaning Tower of Pisa, and a bunch of big skyscrapers. He made it to Rome in two minutes because he was so fast. When he got there he met the coolest and tallest human being he'd ever seen. His name was Air Michael, aka Michael Jordan.

Michael Jordan really liked Mario, and he wanted to take a tour to Italy to meet him. That's why he was in Rome.
Michael Jordan noticed that Steve was warming up his laser eyes, so he walked up to him and said, "Hey, if you want to burn Rome, you have to go through me first. I challenge you to a basketball competition."

Steve had never played basketball before, but he was fast, right? He could jump and fly! There's no way some human, even such a tall one, could beat him.

Michael Jordan tapped a button on the ground with his foot, and a basketball court rose out of the ground.

He clapped his hands and said, "Game on, fella."

They played for an entire two minutes. It was the most impressive, fierce, awesome, radical, and ridiculous game of basketball in the history of all time. It was a CAT-tastrophe.

It came down to the final seconds, but the two players were

locked in a dead tie.

Michael Jordan said, "The next person to score a point wins. Deal?"

"Meow," replied Steve, which in laguar language means: "Bring it."

Steve took the ball and jumped as high as he could. He slammed it so hard that he started an earthquake somewhere else on Earth. Steve was the winner.

Surely Rome was doomed. But no, Steve was so impressed by Michael Jordan's playing that he decided not to destroy the city.

He said, "Michael Jordan, that was a good game. So good that I won't destroy the city, or even the other cities I planned on destroying."

"Thanks," replied Michael Jordan. "You're the man, Steve."

Michael Jordan and Steve went on to create the greatest basketball/crime-fighting team of all time, and together they went back to the jungle and foiled Dr. Fringell's evil plans of Universe domination.

Rescuing Ares

by **Madison Grant, Grade 5**

FROM

Gods and Heroes and Monsters, Oh My!, Summer 2013

Once there lived a demigod. She was a daughter of Ares, god of art and fighting, with the beautiful and singing mom Persephone. Her mom was a mortal and her father was a god. Her name was Classure la Rue.

She was beautiful, with dark brown, very curly hair with light brown highlights. She wore a black biker jacket and black high-heeled boots. She was at one of the most important battles without her father Ares at her side—the battle of going to college. Her father was separated from her when a terrible beast called Levlin, a floating vampire head, took him to the Bermuda Triangle.

Classure lived lonely in a one million dollar house in California with her mom, stepdad, and a cop to protect her from the Levlin. But she had second thoughts about saving her father.

She jet-skied to the Bermuda Triangle with an arrow, bow, phone, and her bike in her motorboat/submarine.

She then learned that she could get through. She called her father and saved him, but then came the Levlin. She grabbed her bomb-arrow and metal bow, killing the Levlin. She and her father arrived home safely, and Ares helped her get through college at Stanford.

Untitled

by **Monzell McKnight, Grade 11**

FROM

Catching Feelings, Winter 2012

So as I was walking to the park with my dad, I saw something hanging from a tree. I went closer for a better look, and I noticed it was a baby lizard. At first glance, I didn't know what type of lizard it was. I grabbed it and showed it to my dad.

"Monzell, you can keep it when we take it to the vet to get it checked out. We have to make sure it doesn't have a disease or anything."

I was so happy. We went straight to the vet to get her checked out, and she didn't have anything at all. They said she was as healthy as a horse.

I ran home with her with excitement. Now it is three years later, and I am fifteen, and she is four. I decided to name her Liz, and I found out that she was an iguana. She was just the best pet that anyone could ask for. She was just so amazing. One day, my big brother, who is five years older than I am, took my PS3 out of my room. When Liz saw from her cage that I was mad, she broke out of it and ran into his room and bit him on the hand and foot. She ran back in my room under my bed so my brother couldn't find her.

"Where is Liz?" he demanded.

"She just ran downstairs, why?" I said.

"She just bit me, that little thing!" he screamed.

About an hour later, she came from under my bed and came to my side.

"Liz, why did you do that? (Even though it was very funny.)"

She looked at me with her head tilted and turned around and slapped me with her tail. She ran back into her cage.

I really miss her, though. She was the one who got me hooked on Oreos. When I was in the grocery store with her, I was walking down the cookie aisle. She saw them and grabbed them with her tail and put them in my hand. I looked at her and asked her if she wanted me to buy them, and surprisingly, she shook her head yes. We got home, and she tore open the pack and had an Oreo. She then started to get excited and happy, so I decided to try one. It was just amazing, and I just loved Oreos from that day. Liz was just the best pet ever. Although she died a month ago, I still remember her nonstop.

An Excerpt from "Enderman"

by **Nathan Ruiz, Grade 5**

FROM

Elementary School Writing Camp, Summer 2012

The zombies ate Mr. Frank and came out unnoticeably. They ate Uncle Bubba.

But thankfully, they did not eat the Enderman, who was yet so quiet, so mysterious. The Enderman was black, like a shadow; quick, like a shadow; and skillful like a shadow in the dark.

Thundar, the Warrior of all Warriors

by *Antonio Doumas, Grade 5*

FROM

Gods and Heroes and Monsters, Oh My!, Summer 2013

Thundar was the bravest, skilled-est sword-fighting man who ever lived. He was to win the war of all worlds.

So Thundar set out for the war. There were the wildest of animals: lions, griffins, dragons, phoenixes, and tigers. All these animals ate most of the men. Then Thundar and the rest of his men headed out onto the battlefield with a loud barbaric roar: "Ahhh!" The men roared with courage, and the trumpets sounded.

They returned home to their families, and the whole town had a party feast. They danced with bears wearing tutus and drank root beer. After the party, they realized they were dancing with bears, so they screamed and jumped into the lake.

The narrator says, "Some heroes! The End. Hey fool, get back here with my wallet! Here we go again. Now it's The End."

port of call

— Section IV —

FUTURE

The Day my iPod Sent Me 10,000 Years Ahead in Time

by Lara Sonuga, Grade 7

———— FROM ————

Flash Fiction, Summer 2013

"Hey, what are you doing up there? Let's go!"

I groan. Dad's been calling me for ten minutes, trying to make me go to the store with him.

"I'm coming!" I lie, flopping down on my bed and sighing.

I hear his footsteps, clomping up the stairs and getting closer with every passing second. My bedroom door flies open and I wince. Dad marches toward me, his face full of anger.

"I've been calling you for ten minutes, and you're still sitting up here with your stupid guitar?"

"Fine. I'm coming," I say, trying not to risk getting my guitar taken away.

"Oh, no, you're not." He wrenches it from my hands, and I

gasp. "You're grounded, young lady. I'm still going to the store, but you are not going anywhere while I'm gone, do you understand?"

"Dad!"

"Understand?" he repeats.

"Fine," I tell him reluctantly.

"Good." He leaves and slams my door shut.

"Fine. Be that way," I mutter, even though there's no one to hear it. Angrily, I wrench open my nightstand drawer and search for my ancient, dinosaur-age iPod. Even though I haven't used it for months, it still has battery life. I plug in my earbuds and turn on a song that I've never seen on it before. It's an odd, electronic song without words. I close my eyes and let my mind wander.

In my head, I picture a secret outdoor space society in another galaxy. Aliens with weirdly shaped heads parade through a futuristic hallway. I can tell they're invading this giant space-ship. They run faster than any human ever will, carrying weapons that don't even exist on Earth. The aliens barge into a room with more sleeping aliens, these ones with perfectly circular heads, three hands, and thin skin that is tinted blue. Except, one of the sleeping aliens doesn't match the others. As the invading species come closer... I can see that it's me.

This is really scary. I open my eyes to turn the music off, but then I realize I'm not in my room anymore—I'm on a spaceship.

Oh no. How is this even possible?

I get really scared when I see the invading aliens start to attack the sleeping aliens. Weapons fly across the room, decap-itated heads roll on the floor, and aliens jump from surface to surface, screaming either cries for help or war cries.

I roll off my alien bed and duck underneath it, shaking with fear and hoping they don't find me. I try to keep telling myself it is just a dream, but I know it's not. This is real. I hear something rustle behind me, so I turn around and come face to face with a hideous creature pointing a futuristic bow and arrow at me.

Black and green dots swirl around my vision. Oh, no. When I get scared, I black out. I get dizzy, and the last thing I see before everything goes black is the alien preparing to attack me.

I Wish

by *Kassandra Virola, Grade 5*
FROM
A Bubble with a Password, Fall 2012

I wish everybody loved Justin Bieber because he does a lot for us. He goes all around the world to do some concerts, he makes watches, shirts, pajamas, necklaces, bracelets, albums, movies, and more. Instead of him making a lot more stuff, maybe we should do something for him, like writing letters telling him our deepest secrets and hobbies.

If I were to hang out with the Biebs, we would go to the park with his friends. He would go on the swings, go on the slides, play hide-and-seek, and more. The park would have a big scary slide, one slide that rolls, some swings, monkey bars, and more.

If I were to sing one of his songs, I would pick the song called "As Long As You Love Me." It's a really good song.

If I were to go on a date with Justin Bieber, I would go to Golden Corral. I would wear a dress on the date, because it's a perfect outfit. The dress would have polka dots, and it would be white. If I were to go to another place on our date, it would be Putting Edge. I would invite some of my friends to the park, like Jazmin, Alexis, and Kira. His friends would come over to the park, too, like Ryan, Jazz, and Nolin. We would go to Walsh Park and play freeze tag.

If Justin Bieber were to sing a song to me at a concert, he would sing "Boyfriend."

My Perfect Car

by **Rowan Mobley, Grade 6**

FROM

A Bubble with a Password, Fall 2012

When I go to college, I want to go to engineering school so I can make my special car. The reason I want to make my special car is because once I was in a car that only had one cup holder in the back. Thankfully, it was only me in the backseat, but if there were more people, there would have been a riot.

The car would have three cup holders in the backseat, because if there are three people in the backseat and there are only one or two cup holders in the backseat, and all of the people want to put their drinks down, only two can. Then disasters can happen. For example, if they want to go to sleep, then they would have to hold their drinks while they sleep, or they just won't go to sleep.

The backseat would be evenly spaced out. Also, the backseat would be as amazing as the front seats. Like the seats would be heated, you would be able to recline the chairs, and you would have the same foot space. This is how I would make my special car. They would be called bubble cars. Instead of gas stations, there would be bubble stations. Instead of the pipe thing, there would be a wand. You wouldn't have to be sixteen years or older to drive a bubble car. You could be eleven years old or older. The world would be a happier place because people would want to go outside and pop the bubbles instead of sitting on the couch and being couch potatoes.

The Magical Adventure: In the Land of Cheeserocks

A Choose-Your-Own-Adventure Story

Continued from page 41

If Mr. Frank asked Uncle Bubba to give him the magical cheese...

Uncle Bubba saw Mr. Frank's house, which was yellow and looked like a cellphone. Mr. Frank offered to trade with Uncle Bubba for the magical cheese. Mr. Frank offered to give Uncle Bubba fake magical cheese that would transport him back to Broccoli World. He said, "Uncle Bubba, would you like some real human food?"

Uncle Bubba responded, "Yes! I will eat all your food!"

Mr. Frank let out a pugnacious evil laugh, cackling like an evil scientist.

*If they made the trade and Uncle Bubba ate the magical cheese immediately, turn to **page 113.***

*If he bent the cheese and found out that it was fake cheese with broccoli inside, turn to **page 51.***

President Diego

by **Diego Delira, Grade 2**
FROM
An Elevator with Different Floors, Winter 2013

How are you? My name is Diego. I'm the president. One of my duties is to name a national day. My national day is "Gift Day." Everyone gives the president gifts.

Untitled

by **Max Hamm, Grade 6**

FROM

Alexander Graham Bell Elementary School, Spring 2013

Once upon a time, there were two friends named Shanaynay and Enip. They were professional dog walkers. They had walked up to eighteen dogs at one time. Every day they walked dogs. They always tried to break their record of eighteen dogs, but for some reason, they couldn't. Then one day, they beat their record and walked too many dogs at one time. This opened a time rift, and they went five hundred years into the future.

Now, the future was not very happy to have Shanaynay and Enip from the past, so it sent many futuristic beings to track them down and dispose of them. When the beings finally found their prey, Shanaynay and Enip were fascinated by the strange organisms' bodies. They were large, bubble-like shapes with no eyes, mouths, arms, or legs. They were basically balls of slime.

Now, the future inhabitants had not known what Shanaynay and Enip looked like, so they did not know that the bubble beings would not be able to apprehend the two human beings. Shanaynay and Enip were told that they must cooperate or else they would be terminated. The two of them just burst out laughing! They just couldn't believe they could and would be taken in by a bunch of slimes. But at that moment, the slimes swallowed them whole, and Shanaynay and Enip just sat inside air bubbles inside of the slimes feeling very sorry for themselves.

Now, you might remember that Shanaynay and Enip had been walking dogs when they had been swallowed by the time rift, and those dogs had run away when they arrived in the future. But, shortly after Shanaynay and Enip were taken hostage by the slimes, the dogs began to follow the slimy trail their walkers' captors had left behind.

When the dogs found Shanaynay and Enip, they were tied up with gooey ropes and were on trial because time traveling was banned in the future, and the slimes didn't believe it had been an accident that they had traveled through time. But, when the futuristic beings saw the dogs, they immediately set Shanaynay and Enip free because the dog was an endangered animal that had the power to save them if they were dying.

Shanaynay and Enip couldn't get back to their time, but they became friends with the future beings and lived happily ever after. They lived the best lives human beings could live. The End!

The Magical Adventure: In the Land of Cheeserocks

A Choose-Your-Own-Adventure Story

Continued from page 109

If they made the trade and Uncle Bubba ate the magical cheese immediately...

Uncle Bubba ate the cheese, and again felt like jumping out of the window. Then he jumped out of the window and burrowed into the ground to reach Mole World. A bunch of moles lived in Mole World, and it was very, very dark. Mole World smelled very stinky and like soil. Uncle Bubba bumped into a stranger and asked, "Excuse me, sir, where am I?"

The stranger responded, "Mole World! Would you like to meet the mayor?" Uncle Bubba said, "Sure!"

Uncle Bubba gave the stranger his hand, and the stranger's hand felt like slimy worms. When they arrived at the Mayor's

Office, Uncle Bubba heard the mayor's voice. The mayor sounded like a loud pig. The office was cold, and worms were flying in from all angles. Uncle Bubba couldn't see where he was walking because it was so dark and he tripped over the worms on the floor. After Uncle Bubba tripped on them, the worms wiggled away. The mayor announced in his deep pig-mole voice, "How did you get to Mole World? Through the ceiling or the door? If you answer incorrectly, there'll be dire consequences."

If Uncle Bubba said, "I came through the door," turn to **page 134.**

If Uncle Bubba said, "I came through the ceiling," turn to **page 154.**

The New Earth

by *Johnny Negron, Grade 10*

FROM

As Long as Squirrels Love Chicken, Spring 2013

As the moon went away and the sun's beams cooled the earth, the Earthlings finally showed their faces above the molten soil. The sky darkened; the day had begun.

It had been forty-five years since the moon and the sun switched places. Some say it was a curse from the gods. Many have questioned this, and some tried to explain it scientifically, to no avail. Nothing was able to explain this calamitous occurrence. Eighty-five percent of the population was wiped out during the instant switch. Luckily, the survivors of the human race were able to adapt, proving to those who'd doubted the chance of survival.

There were approximately eight hours to scavenge food and supplies for the next day. Secret government tunnels built fifty years prior made it easy for survivors to access the surface, but the radiation also made it dangerous.

The hard part, you might ask? Getting back underground

in time, or, well... you're going to be burned to a crisp. It was my brother and my turn to find some sort of nourishment on the surface. We were running low on food, and my mom had to eat the last of it because of her low blood sugar. My brother Daryl wasn't exactly my idol. My mother had to break up our fights because living under the surface of the Earth consumed our bodies of exasperation. I could not stand to work with my brother; his constant ego caused him to believe that he was the dominant person. Sometimes I believed it was just his anger and frustration making him feel that way. He would always bully me, trying to make me a "man."

My daydreaming about our situation was interrupted with our mother calling us over.

"Out of everything left in this world, I'm glad I have the chance to be with my two boys, who I love with all my heart. I consider myself lucky and praise God every day that I can still see your smiles." Our mother was all we had left, and without her we might as well stand on the surface waiting for the moon to shine its rays. Suddenly, my mother threw up the last bit of food we had. "I need my shots! I lost them on the way down here."

My heart froze faster than lightning striking a tree. We were confused, scared, and worried. I told my brother we needed to do something. Fearing for the worst, we left the underground sanctuary with only one hour left to be safely hidden from the moon's rays. There was a Walgreens next to a gas station, two miles away.

How the building still stood with the heat rays from the moon baffled us. The "G" in Walgreens broke off as we approached the decrepit building. The crash sounded like an explosion as the sign hit the cracked asphalt. The once red sign had faded to grey during the midst of the switch. The mechanical doors still worked as we tried to enter. Desperate, we knew we needed to find shots of insulin for our mother or she'd end up like the rest of our family. Jumping over the pharmacy counter, we saw that everything that was once organized was all over the floor.

"Someone was already here," my brother said. Taking a glance at the stopwatch, we still had forty-five minutes left. "Let's take a break for ten minutes," Daryl said.

I wasn't sure if I wanted to give up looking, so I continued to shuffle through the empty boxes in the medicine cabinets.

"John… I'm sorry." Out of all the shuffling, I heard those words come out of Daryl's mouth. Was he hallucinating? I could not believe those words were coming out of his mouth.

"Sorry for what?" I said.

"I'm sorry for being an ass," he said.

Mama always told us never to swear, but I didn't say anything to him. I was still completely shocked by the apology. "What do you mean?" I said.

"I don't want to be seen as an evil figure in your life. I'm older than you, so I'm trying to make you respect me and learn to adapt in this world. I apologize if I came off as mean."

My emotional side took over, and I hugged him, finally realizing that I had a brother! I decided to apologize for being a brat and continued searching for my mother's medicine. We were low on time, so we hurried. As we were about to give up, the last box on the shelf fell over. I approached it slowly, as if our trials would be useless, expecting only to find that there was nothing behind the counter.

"YES," I shouted. There were four shots of insulin. "Time to make our way back."

We stocked up on nearly-expired ravioli and rushed back. The bridge that we used to reach the Walgreens was making loud and unsubtle squeaks. A board broke; we knew we had to run. Halfway down the bridge, the rest fell apart. We were forced to jump!

"On three!"

We jumped with all our might, and the rest of the bridge collapsed as we made it to the other side. The rest of the trip we power-walked and jogged. We glanced at the clock. The stopwatch said only ten minutes left, but we were still a mile away. Failure was running through our minds and our exhausted bodies. The supplies, freshly stocked, left a load that consumed our energy little by little. There was a minute left, but still hundreds of feet left to cover. Little by little, the moonlight slowly crept along the horizon. I made one last dash to the tunnel, which was in sight.

The stopwatch read ten seconds.

9...8...7...6...5...

The final dash of energy, while the light was inches away from our feet.

4...3...2...1

We dove, but it was too late.

— Section V —

WITHIN YOUR CITY

Nutella

by *Xander Cruz, grade 7*

FROM

Let Out Your Inner Slam, Winter 2013

Nutella

You know you want it

Open it up and find the gold seal

The seal that holds your suspense

Rip it with a fork because you're too excited

Let the life flow out

Stand back and let the rainbows shoot about

Pull out your bread

Smear it all over

While you have no clue that the bread is enjoying this even more
than you

There is no disclaimer about the awesomeness

you might need to sue

Enter it into your mouth

and pay no attention to the angels frolicking on your tongue

Enter it into the wrong tube and the deliciousness might burst a lung

Contain yourself now, no need to drool

Before you know it you'll have a pool

of Nutella. Swimming in it

There is not a single rule

Let the Nutella take over your stomach

and feel as it becomes king

All it needs is a throne and a diamond ring.

Eat another spoonful and there will be two kings

This cannot happen

For the two kings will fight

and you will feel the pain.

You might have to sit down

But you cannot contain the energy

So you lift into the air

your hair is floating everywhere

This is Nutella

But now you drop back to the ground

And realize the jar is empty

So your eyes sink back into your face, shut like they've been

sprayed with mace, you have to go to the store now, this

has turned into a race slow yourself

down as you pace

calm down

it's you who ate it all

and you're to blame
your mum knocks on the door
You open it for her
And you remember
how you ate it all
you've hit a brick wall
As your mom settles down
she says "stop hopping around,
and go make me some toast with Nutella."
You shift from side to side
and wonder what to say
what can you say
what can you do
To take your way
and admit it's true
Your face turns blue as you tell
your mum you ate it all
your face turns red as your
mum tells you to go to bed
So you sleep in shame, knowing
you're to blame
for eating all the Nutella
So the next day you
casually walk over to the store
and get some more.
PROBLEM SOLVED

A Monster

by Marlon Guarad, Grade 1

FROM

Elementary School Writing Camp, Summer 2013

One day a flying car ran out of gas. The flying car fell down to the train tracks. There was a monster in the flying car. He jumped out of the flying car and then went to eat six icicles. He said, "Iciccccccclllllleeeeeeeeeessssssssss." Then he softly said, "Icicles." Then he fell asleep.

Cold Cup, Warm Heart

by Izzy Bell, Grade 9

FROM

As the Door Gradually Opened, Summer 2013

She walked into the neighborhood coffee shop. Ding! Ding!

The barista's eyes flickered towards the door as he heard the familiar bell chime. The chime startled him, making him drop the wooden Ticonderoga pencil he had been using to finish his seemingly impossible crossword, for the coffee shop closed in ten minutes and he usually didn't get customers this late.

She took a few steps forward once in the coffee shop, her pale blue eyes squinting through light and frosty eyelashes as she sized up the menu. What did she want?

Something cold, she thought. *Something really, really cold.*

A sudden chill coursed through her body, causing her to shiver. She subconsciously rubbed her hands together, the wool fabric of her red mittens slowly thawing out her hands, warming her. Frustrated, she pulled her hands apart and kept them still at her sides, refusing to let the heat of her mittens numb her cold fingers.

The first thing she noticed was the jazz music playing, typically masked by the chatter of customers enjoying their cups of coffee.

For some reason, knowing she was the only one here on this cold winter's day comforted her. She took a deep breath, in through her nose and out through her mouth. The first real breath, she realized, that she had taken all day. The next thing she couldn't help but notice was the barista looking at her, almost admiring her through his deep, chocolate-brown eyes. He looked unkempt to her, his short brown hair a little too scruffy for her liking. She walked up to the counter, and after a final glance at the menu through scowled brows, came to a decision she was satisfied with.

"Iced Moch-ch-cha," she said to the barista, talking through chattering teeth.

"It's freezing outsi-"

"I didn't ask for the weather forecast, I just want my d-damn drink."

The barista took a moment just then and really looked at this pathetic woman standing before him. This beautiful woman with rosy red cheeks and chapped pink lips. This miserable woman ordering cold coffee on one of the coldest days of the year. This fragile woman having trouble accepting kindness, regardless of the sincerity. A knot of thick rope tightened in his stomach as he realized he felt sorry for this poor woman. Even more sorry than he had felt for himself working now seventeen minutes past his shift.

A crumpled five-dollar bill was thrown onto the counter, and before the barista could tell her the iced mocha was only $3.25, she snarled, "Keep the change, Buddy."

With a quick flip of her tangled, auburn hair, she turned away from him, and only then did the barista realize he didn't catch her name.

"Name, Miss?"

Without turning around she called, "Mandy. M-A-N-D-Y," spelling it out for him as if he was incapable of sounding out letters himself.

"I'm Scott."

"Whatever."

Only after she walked away did Mandy realize he didn't need to know her name if no one else was there.

The barista continued to watch Mandy, completely infatuated with her. He watched this beautiful woman whisk away bangs that would stubbornly fall over her eyes. He watched this miserable woman weaken her posture, deflate, and collapse as she slumped down onto the cushioned chair seated next to the four-panel frosted window. He watched as this fragile woman closed her eyes and took deep breaths, in through her nose,and back out through her mouth, over and over.

He wrote down her name in smooth cursive on the coffee cup and proceeded to watch this woman he had never seen before sit in his coffee shop, now twenty minutes past closing time.

God, my life is a mess, Mandy thought. It had been a long day. She slumped down on a comfy chair, looking out the window, her contacts blurring as reluctant tears welled in her eyes.

"This guy better hurry up with my drink," she mumbled almost inaudibly as she sniffed back the tears that were on the verge of pouring down her cheeks like angry waterfalls. Exhausted from the day, she let herself close her eyes, the intoxicating aroma of coffee beans filling her nose and making her dizzy; she slipped into unconsciousness.

"Mandy!"

Suddenly jolted awake, she pulled herself up off the chair and groggily stumbled towards the counter.

"Thanks." She stifled a yawn.

Mandy reached out a hand for her drink and was taken aback when the barista hesitated before giving it to her. After a few awkward seconds, he calmly placed the drink in her extended hand. Irritated, she waited for him to say something along the lines of "Have a nice night" or "Thanks for coming by." but instead he just smiled at her; a huge, goofy grin that reached ear to ear. Deciding she didn't have the time or the energy to contemplate the meaning of that smile, she walked hastily out of the coffee shop hearing the "Ding! Ding!" behind her as the door slammed shut.

Mandy walked back out of the coffee shop into the frozen landscape that was her reality, bringing her iced coffee to her lips for a sip. She should have known something was wrong the moment the barista gave her a drink that warmed her red wool mittened hands rather than preserving their numbness.

She glanced down at the cup.

Written on it, in smooth cursive writing, was this:

Mandy,
It's cold out there.
Stay warm.
-S

Mandy glanced back at the coffee shop and began to make her way back, feeling the frustration and aggravation she had kept inside all day course through her veins like blood when she noticed the "CLOSED" sign hung on the front door, the freezing snow already forming icicles around its wooden edges.

She stopped in her tracks. Taking a deep breath, in through her nose and out through her mouth, Mandy put the hot coffee to her lips, closing her eyes and allowing the heat rising from the cup to warm her, comfort her. Mandy stood there in front of the neighborhood coffee shop on that cold winter's day and drank the whole thing.

Inside Trains

by *Amalia Pappa, Grade 5*

FROM

Poetry Bump!, Summer 2013

YOLO
you only live
once
said Abby
as she jumped into the pool
from
the garage roof.
When she got
dry
her friend said
I'll walk you home.
After walking
for miles
her friend said
where do you live?
Abby said,
I live inside
trains.

An Accident

by **Josh Broemer, Grade 7**

FROM

Poetry Bump!, Summer 2013

I forgot to lock the door today.

Someone got in...

and ate your favorite cheese.

It totally wasn't me

I guess you never know what you have until it's gone

Sorry

by JJ Shankar and Daniel Dardon, Grades 8 and 6

FROM

Poetry Bump!, Summer 2013

Sorry I pulled that seat from under you

But to be honest

Does it really hurt to fall on the floor

The Magical Adventure: In the Land of Cheeserocks

A Choose-Your-Own-Adventure Story

Continued from page 114

If Uncle Bubba said, "I came through the door,"...

Uncle Bubba said, "The door."
"Wrong, kill him," said Zack Affron, the mayor. Two moles walked up to him and beheaded him. Then the mayor ate his head and got transported to Marshmallow World. Zack started eating marshmallows like crazy. Marshmallows were falling from the sky like snowflakes on a snowy day. He was so happy he shaved his hair off.

Ending by Harry Biggerman, Grade 4

Uncle Bubba was nervous to say "Door," and he should have been! Uncle Bubba said, "Door," and the mole mayor shouted.

"That is impossible!" the mole mayor shouted. "Only moles can come through the door! But you have answered incorrectly. Throw him in the pit!"

Uncle Bubba was seized by the arms and thrown down the hole where he desperately tried to get out. So, know when you hear the rustling of grass, it is Uncle Bubba trying to get out of the hole.

Ending by Penelope Huang, Grade 3

Dear Mint

by *Maurice Oldham, Grade 3*

FROM

There I Am Looking at You with a Hungry Face, Spring 2013

Dear Mint,

I am inviting you to a fight. I am tired of being on the top of the Girl Scout cookie. I want to be inside of the cookie because on the bottom it is freezing, and in the summer it is too hot outside.

Meet me at the steel cage. I am going to take pieces off of me and throw them at you. The only rule is: climb over the cage, but don't let your opponent do it first.

Don't get too close to me, because we don't like each other's smell. You smell terrible—so very bad—that it feels like fire, and I melt from your smell. Despite that, I can get back up in thirty seconds.

I am inviting all my relatives. You'd better not get close to them. We're going to be inside of the cookie, not you! It will feel make me feel better. If I stay on the outside, I'll melt. And it's not fair to me to stay on the outside.

This fight will take place in the middle of the street. It will be the last fight. This has been going on for centuries. This needs to end!

From your opponent,
Chocolate

P.S. You'd better come!

They Won't Lobotomize You

by **Kennedy Ward, Grade 10**
——————— FROM ———————
Science that Matters, Fall 2012

After living sixteen years on Earth, I think that it's understandable that I've come to the conclusion that I have a tendency of saying and doing things that people don't find socially acceptable. For example, I don't believe women should be pressured into taking priority in doing the cooking and the cleaning in the household. I don't cook. I don't clean. Anyone in my house knows that it's a very rare occasion for me to turn on a stove for anything besides boiling water. I despise cooking. It accumulates dirty dishes, sparks the opportunity for spills, and it's just too much of a hassle for me.

I have certain beliefs on cleaning, also. I believe that whoever made it dirty should be the one to make it clean. Plain and simple. Of course, this is not how things operate in my house, but this is just me dreaming of my perfect world. My mother likes to describe me as being "a good kid, but rebellious."

Luckily for me, it's 2012 and it's perfectly okay for me to be this way. It's who I am. However, in 1960, this was the exact type of attitude that earned twelve-year-old Howard Dully an icepick lobotomy.

Howard Dully was a fairly normal young boy. He enjoyed riding his bike and playing chess. Like most children, Dully had his moments of rebellion. His stepmother thought Howard was "defiant." According to Walter Freeman, the infamous American physician who specialized in lobotomy, the young Dully "turns the room's lights on when there is broad sunlight outside." Freeman's psychiatric notes on Howard Dully also describe the boy as being a daydreamer and objecting to going to bed. This behavior is what led Dully's father and stepmother to allow Freeman to perform an icepick lobotomy on the young boy.

Walter Freeman's ice pick lobotomy was a ghastly procedure to watch. The psychosurgeon would use electricity to render his patients unconscious. According to National Public Radio's website, Freeman would then "take a sharp ice pick-like instrument and insert it above the patient's eyeball through the orbit of the eye, into the frontal lobes of the brain, moving the instrument back and forth. Then he would do the same thing on the other side of the face." The purpose of Freeman's lobotomy was to cut the prefrontal lobe, the region of the brain that controls most of a person's behavior and personality, and the patient would be relieved of his mental disorder.

Based on psychiatrist John Pippard's personal studies of hundreds of British neurosurgeon Sir Wylie McKissock's lobotomy patients, one third of the patients benefited from the surgery, one third got worse after the surgery, and a third showed no effects at all. According to Howard Dully, his lobotomy affected his spirit and made him feel like "a freak [and] ashamed." Despite these inconsistent results, more than 18,000 lobotomies were performed between 1851 and 1939, as stated in cerebromente.org, an electronic magazine dedicated to neuroscience.

The Soviet Union viewed the lobotomy as being an immoral practice and banned the procedure in the 1940s. Lobotomies became less popular in the 1950s, but they were still performed on a few patients. The lobotomy's decreasing popularity was a result of the introduction of drugs such as Thorazine that could be used as antipsychotic treatments.

Nevertheless, methods of psychosurgery are still in existence today. According to a paper in The Dartmouth Undergraduate Journal of Science (DUJS Online), the Anterior Capsulotomy is used to treat OCD. Deep Brain Stimulation (DBS) consists of the surgeon inserting an electrode into the patient's brain. This procedure has been used to treat Parkinson's disease and is currently being tested in clinical trials as a treatment for depression. In modern-day America, psychosurgery is considered a last-resort treatment for patients with mental disorders.

In addition to contemporary medical procedures that prevent barbaric operations like the lobotomy from being a popular form of treatment for "disorderly" people, I believe that psychosurgery has dwindled in prevalence largely due to the world's recent acceptance of people being different from one another. President

Obama has publicly stated that he is a supporter of gay marriage, making him the first American president to do so. Hip-hop artist and R&B singer-songwriter Frank Ocean recently announced that he is bisexual, despite the fact that the genres are known for their heteronormativity and sometimes homophobic lyrics. This Wednesday, Dan Cathy, president of the Chick-fil-A fast-food chain, expressed his stance against same-sex marriage. It's plain to see that the people of America have the freedom to say and do what they please and don't always have to agree with one another's ideas. Up until 1954, schools were still racially segregated. That was only a mere fifty-eight years ago.

I feel that so many people take their brand-new freedom for granted. Many of us sit and complain about how we have the desire for political and social changes that will benefit one another, but we never put those words into action. We no longer have to worry about being put in straightjackets and having our brains picked apart just because we think and act differently. We have no reason to be afraid anymore. It's okay to speak up, so why don't you?

How Crocghostee Came to Be

by **Cole Harris**, *grade 3*

FROM

Elementary School Writing Camp, Summer 2012

One day, Marcus McBooty was walking in the park on the way to work as a captain on a boat when a bird swooped down and pooped on his head.

"Hey!" he screamed. "What was that for?"

He walked away furiously and murmured, "Stupid bird."

The bird's eyes glowed red and he flew directly at Marcus. Quickly, Marcus picked up a large, shiny black rock and threw it at the bird. The bird took a direct hit and it fell to the ground. Marcus assumed it was dead, because the wings were off the bird, and a bird couldn't be a bird without wings. But boy was he wrong!

The wings started to flop and Marcus's mouth hung open. The bird flew directly into his mouth.

"EWW!" he screamed and yelled something that made the

woman next to him gasp. He started to walk, but floated. He kept walking, and flew up fifty feet!

He screamed, "AHH!" and then yelled "I CAN FLY, I CAN FLY!"

Everyone in the park looked up to see; closed their eyes for five seconds, rubbing them; looked up again; and, screaming, ran away.

"Aww," he said miserably. And he kept on walking to work. When he got to the ship, it was empty.

"Of course," he said. "Always the first one here." He flew over into his office.

A Banana Split = Fruit Mix

by Students in Mrs. Nelson's 7th Grade Class

FROM

Hiram H Belding Elementary School, Winter 2012

"Ahhhhh!" shouted Bobby. Unlike an ordinary morning, he woke up, went to the bathroom, and saw the most frightening thing. He found himself peeling.

Eleven-year-old Bobby was a banana. He'd never seen anyone like him peel before.

"Oh my, what will the other kids at school think? I've never peeled before."

He slowly crept into his sister's room, looking for her Fabulous Banana makeup kit. He heard his sister coming up the stairs. She was so close that he had no choice but to hide under the bed.

"Mom, oh no. Where's my makeup kit? Did you take my

makeup again?" the sister yelled down the stairs.

After she left, Bobby opened the makeup kit and found Banana Balm lip-gloss, Banana style powder, and the Best of Bananas for Lashes eyelash curler. He started putting on the Banana style powder to cover up the fact that he was peeling. He looked in the mirror and saw that it worked.

He screamed, "Yes, it worked! Oops, that was too loud."

Panicking, he heard his sister's steps while he ran towards his room.

"Haha. You are going through this stage, too. Let me help you," said Ashley, his older sister. After she was done putting on his makeup, Bobby realized he was late for school and ran out of the house.

The bell rang and Bobby ran into his classroom. Not noticing that his makeup smeared, the class gasped at Bobby's appearance. The class started to gasp. He sat down and put his book over his face. He looked over and saw the new fruit, Steve the orange, copying him.

"Stop copying me," he whispered.

The teacher, a pineapple named Mrs. Solis said, "Is there anything you would like to share with the class?"

"No," the orange replied.

The banana peeked over and said, "You're peeling just like me."

"Don't worry, you're not alone. You can stay with me today," the orange said to the banana.

The rest of the week, the banana peeled along with the orange. By Friday, at first period, Grape and Apple, the popular kids, stopped them and asked what was happening to their skin.

"We're peeling," explained Bobby.

"I wish we could peel too. That is straight up swag," said the popular group.

Later during the day, they found peels all over the bathroom floor.

"Steve, what's going on?"

They walked out of the bathroom together, finding nothing but peeled fruit in the hallway.

Find Out Why!

by Jocelyn Ortega, grade 5

———————————— FROM ————————————

They Want to Kiss the Sidewalk, Fall 2011

Have you ever wondered why leaves change colors? The answer is that green means young leaves, yellow means ten to fifty years old, and red or brown means fifty to one hundred years. Green is in the spring. Dark green is in the summer. Red or brown are in the fall, and no leaves are in winter.

For the leaves, a year is one day. The leaves fall down from the trees because they want to kiss the sidewalk and want to go trick-or-treating. All the leaves jump on each other and turn into a giant leaf, and then they follow the trick-or-treaters.

Expensive Names

*by **Danyelle Patton, Grade 10***

FROM

As Long as Squirrels Love Chicken, Spring 2013

Babies are expensive!

Over the last fourteen years, there has been a study going on focusing on the names of babies. Since the U.S. has been sixteen trillion dollars in debt, parents have become broke and are naming their kids expensive things they can't afford. The most common names are Diamond, Pearl, Mercedes, Alexis, Porsha, Paris, London, Crystal, Armani, and Tiffany. There are twins called Range and Rover. Also there are triplets called Polo, Ralph, and Lauren. Note that all of these are expensive. Now, these kids with expensive names can't live up to their names; consequently, they have to settle with poverty.

Savannah Collins, parent of the triplets Polo, Ralph, and Lauren, proclaimed, "I may not have money, but I named my kids 'expensive' names hoping they would turn out like what their names symbolize."

Dr. Webster, a specialist in psychology, says, "Parents who name their kids expensive names are often unsatisfied with their financial standards, so they use their kids to escape their pain. The names aren't effective because the kids don't represent what their names are. The kids are feeling used from their parents not being able to buy expensive things and using them for comfort."

These kids have been followed throughout their lives, and we noticed that they actually didn't amount to their names. The twins Range and Rover are both in jail for grand theft auto, because they were tired of taking public transportation. Polo, Ralph, and Lauren are all wearing Aeropostale. All of the kids are now suffering from broke-a-titis, a disease where people don't have enough money, and are considered "broke."

The Holiday Squeeze

by **Dametrius Coleman, Grade 11**

FROM

Catching Feelings, Winter 2012

Money. Got to make enough. Because my girl thinks she wants a Coach purse. Do you know how much a Coach purse costs?

Times like this I wish Santa really existed. If he did exist, I would certainly put a Coach purse on his list. But how do I get my hands on that list? You know Santa's got bodyguards, right? But I'm thinking, maybe, dress as an elf....Use my elf disguise to sneak into this ice factory in the North Pole. So, now I'm in there—I see elves skating around with red present boxes with green bows. I see some carry presents shaped like octagons. All I could think was, "How do they wrap that?" But anyway, back to my girlfriend and that Coach purse....

First time she showed it to me, we were at her house on the computer, and I can still remember, she said, "I want to show you something." As soon as she typed the first word, "Coach," my heart started racing. I remember I wanted to tell her right then that there was no way possible that was going to happen. But....

Then I remembered Mr. D telling me about this writing contest at school. He said, in a smart way (he's real smart), first place was $250. I thought, "BAM! $250! That's all I need." But I told my girl, while we were sitting there at her computer, I told her, "Umm, Tyler, you might want to have a backup plan because financially, in these hard times, my allowance is unstable."

She looked at me and said, "It's okay."

So I was off the hook in a way but secretly still wanted to surprise her. I knew I had to get that money by winning the writing contest.

The contest was all about kinship. I had to show a moment of kinship in the best possible way. And it just so happened that the perfect moment had come two weeks before, at a funeral. When I say "perfect," I don't mean "happy." I mean perfect as in I'd recently been thinking about kinship-type ideas.

So I started to write about it down in the back of the basement at my family's house while my brothers were watching Monday Night Football up front.

It amazed me how so many ideas and thoughts came out so fast. I wrote and wrote.

I went to school the next day. Turned it in. Got it back. Got ready to do a second draft after my basketball game after school... But then, middle of the game, I got the hardest foul EVER and broke my thumb. Now when I type, that thumb comes in handy. You got the space bar, that's on the thumb. You got the mouse, thumb's job. Without the thumb, my typing looked like alphabet soup.

Suddenly that picture in my head of me and Tyler and the Coach purse making a happy family turned into a broken home. But then, I had to tell my thumb, "Suck it up, thumb!" And believe it or not, a week later I'm on my third draft. As for my thumb, he's just the Kobe Bryant of thumbs. He plays hurt.

We'll just have to see if Mr. KBOT (Kobe Bryant of Thumbs) can make my holiday squeeze a holiday miracle...

The Magical Adventure: In the Land of Cheeserocks

A Choose-Your-Own-Adventure Story

Continued from page 114

If Uncle Bubba said, "I came through the ceiling,"...

He came through the ceiling. The mayor said, "Good job." Then he went through a portal to the real world.

Ending by Auguste Chase, Grade 4

———

Uncle Bubba got famous because he teleported to a magical land. He also got famous because he wrote a book about his adventure. It was called, "The Magical Adventure."

Ending by Nico Aleman, Grade 4

The Superheroes of Shaing Song

by Breanna Blue, Markel Smith, Destiny James, Malaysia Howard, Tamika Smith, and Damarreon Warfield, Grade 8

——————————— FROM ———————————

Nicholson Technology Academy, Spring 2013

Once upon a time, there was a dog named Oreo. Oreo was a black and white dog that could fly and shoot fudge from his eyes. His wings were vanilla colored. He had a friend named Jimmie Philip. Jimmie Philip was a brown kangaroo with a red nose and a white pouch. Jimmie Philip had the amazing ability to jump. He could jump from world to world, bringing Oreo with him in his pouch. Everyone knew they were best friends because of a "Best Friends" necklace that they each wore. If Jimmie ever needed Oreo, he would jump so hard that the world shook. When Oreo needed Jimmie, he would bark loud enough that Jimmie could hear him anywhere in the universe.

They lived in the city Shaing Song. They both lived together in an apartment on the fifteenth floor with no doors. They would just jump or fly into the windows. Though, all around the world they had secret lairs under trees. They would touch the trees and go underground.

Meanwhile, there was a big evil lion named Larry. He was the most evil lion in the world. He went around the world stealing from every bank he saw.

One day, Jimmie Philip and his mom were going to the bank to get money for college. Jimmie left to use the bathroom when all of the sudden Larry the Lion burst into the door. He had such a big belly that it touched the ground. His stripes were red and purple, the red matching the red of his glowing eyes.

"ME-ow! I mean, ROAR! I'm Larry the Lion. Give me all your money!" growled Larry.

Larry snatched the money from Jimmie's mom and ran out of the bank, jumping on his moped. He rode off with all the money. Jimmie came back from the bathroom.

His mom cried, "Jimmie! Jimmie! Someone took all of our money! I'm going to call the kangaroo police!"

Jimmie replied, "Don't worry, Mom. I got this."

Jimmie tore off his clothes, revealing his superhero uniform. He jumped with all of his might straight through the ceiling and out onto the street. When he landed, the world shook like an earthquake. He knew that he needed Oreo.

Oreo was at home playing with his dog bone when he started to feel the earth shake. "Jimmie!" he thought. Oreo flew as fast as he could to meet Jimmie at the bank.

Oreo flew and broke through the bank's window.

"What's wrong, Jimmie?" asked Oreo.

"A big fat lion just stole all of my tuition money!"

"What's tuition money?" Oreo asked.

"It's the money I need to go to college! And we have to go get it!" yelled Jimmie.

"You're right!" said Oreo.

Oreo jumped into Jimmie's pouch and they started jumping from city to city, looking for Larry's moped. Finally, they found a trail of money that was falling from Larry's moped. They followed the fallen money straight to Larry, who was robbing another bank.

"STOP!" yelled Oreo and Jimmie.

Oreo shot fudge from his eyes on the road in front of Larry's moped and into Larry's eyes. Larry slipped and slid, falling off of his moped into a pool of fudge. As he fell, the money flew into the air. Jimmie jumped and caught the money before it fell into all the fudge.

Just then, a curly-haired old lady walked up, knitting a sweater for her pet cat.

"Have you seen my pet cat, Fluffy?" asked the old lady.

Larry looked up and tried to run away, but the fudge was too slippery. He just fell and slipped. The old lady noticed Larry.

"Fluffy! It's you!" cried the old lady. "I've missed you! Where have you been?"

She scooped him up into her arms and carried Fluffy off to take him back home.

"Woah! Wasn't expecting that... He was just a giant cat called Fluffy," said Oreo.

Oreo and Jimmie looked at each other and started laughing while Fluffy looked back over the shoulder of the old lady, heading back to his real home, defeated.

Telekinesis Within Sanitation Worker

by **Yu Jing Chen, Grade 6**

FROM

Skinner West Elementary School, Spring 2012

One day, a long time ago, there lived a lonely sanitation worker. He lived with his parents in a run-down, dull, dingy, and dark apartment.

One day, as he was trudging his way to work, his friend, the dim-witted Fred, cried, "Look, Morris!" in his squeaky, duck-like voice. Morris wiped the sweat from his furry brow and brushed his brown hair back, trying to make it spiky. However, it stayed as flat as always.

Fred cried again, "LOOK!" Morris swiveled his head around and was about to say, "Be quiet, Fred!" in his grumpy voice but what he saw was too strange. Morris stepped closer to Fred's shrimpy silhouette. Warily, he looked up and saw a glowing green tub of goo.

"What in the world is that?" Morris asked in his raspy but quiet voice.

Fred whispered, "I dunno but it sure does look yummy. Do you wanna try it?"

Morris looked at Fred curiously and whispered back, "That is so disgusting! But then again...now that I think about it, it looks like my mom's lasagna."

The two idiotic sanitation workers went up to the tub full of goo, each step full of suspense. The odor from the alley drifted into their noses. When they reached the tub, Fred didn't look back but Morris considered it for a second. Fred drank it and said, with his mouth full, "Hmmm, not bad."

Morris hesitantly sipped some and immediately felt like he was eating the richest and best chocolate in the world. Morris exclaimed, "This is some GOOD stuff" and gobbled some more down. Little did they know the goo was actually toxic waste, which was capable of giving them powers like no other. Soon enough, Morris and Fred started to feel a tingly feeling and felt funny. Morris suddenly discovered that he had telekinesis and Fred discovered that he could sing like there was no tomorrow. Morris suddenly was able to lift the tub of goo and place it right into his hands.

As Morris and Fred turned around to test their powers on other stuff, their garbage truck came speeding by. Trash flew almost everywhere and bits of banana fell into Morris's flat, brown hair. The grimy truck brushed by them and Fred screamed in an operatic voice, "Help! Our truck!" Morris, angry that his hair was ruined, stopped the truck with telekinesis and left it floating in midair.

The bad guy, confused and afraid, peered outside the truck and frantically screamed. He held onto his seat like a coward and as if the wind was going to tear him away and down to the awaiting ground below. The bad guy shouted in a quivery voice, "Help! I'll do anything if you let me go!"

Morris shouted, "No thank you" and handed his cell phone to Fred. Fred fumbled with the phone and finally called the police.

Fred sang, "Help! Bad guy tried to take our truck! We're at 1234 South Sesame Street!"

Fred was frustrated because the police thought he was just a joke. As Fred made the call, Morris observed the bad guy. The bad guy peered down and Morris caught a glimpse of his face. Along with an eye patch, he had an extremely crooked nose with a wart on the tip, a scar on his right cheek, a tattoo that said, "I luv mom" and a buff body. He was nearly bald and was tall.

A few minutes later, a group of bald policemen came. Right then, Morris moved the truck back on the ground and right as he managed to escape, the police grabbed him. Right as they laid their eyes on the bad guy, they exclaimed, "That's him! It's Ricardo! How'd you fellas manage to catch him?"

Morris shrugged and said in his quiet voice, "Luck?"

Ricardo screamed, "The truck! It was flying! They're sorcerers! Evil sorcerers I tell you!"

The police dragged him away and looked at him as though he was a lunatic and said to Morris and Fred, "Sorry boys. Fifty years in jail will do him good. Thank you for your help."

Soon after, Morris and Fred were broadcast on TV and were featured in the newspaper. Most of the time, Fred was busy observing the TV set to answer any questions, and any time he was asked directly, he would be lost and just nod, smile, and say yes. Morris, who was the shy kind just sat and stared at the floor most of the time. The most that they got out of either of them was a single word, "Luck", and occasionally "Magic" from Fred. In the newspapers, Fred was always smiling in the opposite direction and Morris was captured at an awkward moment, like when he was telling Fred to turn around.

Soon, they were famous everywhere. They were heroes and Ricardo was arrested and charged for many crimes. Why did he decide to steal a garbage truck? Nobody knows. Ricardo was wanted in more than ten cities, and for capturing him, Morris and Fred each received $5,000,000. Morris used the money to move out of his parents' apartment and Fred, who was still stupid, spent the money on Kleenex for no reason at all. Morris now owns a gigantic, five-story mansion that is bright purple.

An Open Letter to the Person I Lend Pencils To

by *Rene Martinez-Salas, Grade 12*

FROM

As Long as Squirrels Love Chicken, Spring 2013

Dear Person I Lend Pencils To,

Here. Have another one. It's not like I buy them. No, my dad owns a whole store of school supplies. No, really, I own the whole pencil business. Yeah, okay, I have pencils to spare. I have so many I give them away. Ask me every day for one. Okay, bro, it's cool that at home you have a whole collection. It does not matter to me, not one bit, not at all.

The Amazing Tortilla Chef

by **The Students in Mrs. Riefenberg's 4th Grade Class**

FROM

Mitchell Elementary School, Spring 2013

In the middle of the night, Michael, a tortilla chef who was getting ready for his night shift, went to Dunkin' Donuts to buy a vanilla latte. His white pants and white apron were a little cold in the chilly night, but he felt good because he was wearing his lucky underwear. He unlocked his jumping kangaroo bike from the box he kept it in in the basement. It started jumping all over the place. He got his lasso, swung it, and caught the bike around the tire. He pulled himself onto the bike and started it jumping towards coffee and work.

It was a five-mile ride to the gas station with the Dunkin' Donuts in it, but he really needed a large vanilla latte before work. It was going to be a long night. He was going to have to make one hundred and six tortillas before this night was through. The streets were empty, except maybe for criminals, and the street lights were flickering all around him, but he was not scared. He was the bravest and the strongest tortilla chef in all the world.

His shift started at 9:00 p.m., and he only had 49 minutes before he had to be at work. He pulled his jumping bike into the gas station, and he had no idea that a criminal lurked in the shadows...

Michael got off his bike and locked it to the gate. "Don't jump away, okay? I need you later!" he said as he pulled a carrot out of his pocket and fed it to the bike. The kangaroo bike happily chewed the carrot, smiled, and wagged its back tire. Michael walked into Dunkin' Donuts and saw that his friend Gerry was working that night.

"Hey Gerry!" Michael said. "What's up? Has it been a busy night tonight?"

Gerry shook his head. "It's been really slow. I've been alone here all day. I thought I saw someone lurking in the shadows outside, maybe wearing a black hoodie? I don't know. Did you see anything out there?"

"No, I haven't seen anyone. It's really dark, though. Maybe I just couldn't see." Michael said.

"Okay," said Gerry. "Are you going to work? Do you need some coffee?"

"Oh yeah. Give me my favorite. The largest vanilla latte ever."

Gerry said, "Okay, it'll take a few minutes, but it's coming right up."

Michael looked out into the dark parking lot, looking to see if there was anyone lurking out there, but instead of a criminal in a black hoodie, he saw a beautiful, if not a little suspicious-looking, lady walking across the parking lot. She was wearing lots of sparkly jewelry, a fur coat (or maybe two?) and a very pretty top hat.

She pushed open the door. The bell above the door jingled, and Gerry turned to greet her.

"Evening, ma'am. Need some coffee?"

"No," she said in a high, funny-sounding voice, "I just came in to see if you had seen the news? There is a criminal on the loose! Check the nightly news!"

Gerry and Michael turned on the news and got distracted. This criminal had been stealing jewelry, fur coats, and other disguises all over the city all day long. He had escaped ten policemen and four police dogs, and now he was believed to be hungry and thirsty. The friends were so busy watching the news they didn't even notice that the suspicious lady was getting closer and closer to the counter.

Then, she took Michael's coffee and filled her purse with chocolate donuts, honey donuts with chocolate chips, munchkins, and cookies. She was about to make her getaway when Michael said, "Oh, by the way, how much do I owe you for that coffee?"

Gerry looked at the counter where the coffee should be and said, "Where is it?! I just put it right there!"

The mysterious woman called from by the door, "Tootle-oo! Bye! Hope they catch that criminal!" in her high, strange voice. She opened the door and left. As the little bell jingled again, Michael said to Gerry, "Did that lady look a little funny to you?"

Gerry said, "Yeah...she did. Come to think of it, she looked a lot like that criminal on TV. Maybe she's his sister."

"Maybe," said Michael, "But didn't they say the criminal was around here? And he was hungry and thirsty?"

"And that he had stolen lots of fur coats and jewelry!" said Gerry. "Well, I'll make you another latte, because I know you've got a long night tonight, and I don't want you to get fired."

"Not tonight, Gerry. I think I know exactly where that criminal is, and I want my coffee back. I'll talk to you later, but for now, call the police and tell them I'm on the case!"

Michael busted open the doors, unlocked his kangaroo bike, and said, "C'mon bike, we've got a criminal to catch. I'm feeling very brave tonight, and with your help and my lucky underwear, we're going to catch this guy and get my coffee back!"

The bike hopped the greatest hop it had ever hopped, and Michael saw the glittering jewelry the criminal was wearing just up ahead. He pulled out his lasso and swung it right at the criminal. It looped right around his shoulders and pinned his arms right to his sides. By the time Michael got the criminal, he had dropped the chocolate donut he had been eating, but the latte was still in his hands, completely full.

The criminal said, "AAAAGGGGGRRRRRRRHHHHHHH," but it didn't sound anything like a lady this time.

Michael said, "I knew it! You are the criminal! This is one crime you won't get away with today. Give me that coffee!"

He grabbed the warm cup right out of the criminal's hands, locked him to the nearest telephone pole, pulled out his cell phone, and told the police where they could find the criminal. Then he hopped on his kangaroo bike one more time and made it to work right on time. He had one hundred and six tortillas to make tonight, after all.

When he walked through the doors at work, his boss said, "Hey Michael, how's it going?"

Michael said, "Pretty good. I caught a criminal AND I got my coffee. What more could you want?"

The End

—— Section VI ——

WITHIN YOURSELF

Untitled

by **Jaxanna Fink, Grade 6**

FROM

Alexander Graham Bell Elementary School, Spring 2013

There once was a man named Lest.
Through his life he was very depressed.
He devoured some snacks,
And away went his slacks,
And just like a woman he was dressed.

Lest was a very nice man.
He owned a large minivan.
He misses his wife
Who has no more life
So now he lives with his Gram.

He opened his fridge and found cheese.
He ate the whole thing with ease.
"This doesn't taste right,"

He said with great fright
And then looked down at his knees.
He was wearing a dress and high heels.
They were made from the skin of gold eels.
He had a large boa
The color of Coca-Cola
And had jewelry the color of teal.

There was great shock on his glorious face.
"For now I shall call myself Grace."
He realized he loved it,
Felt his hair and he rubbed it,
And no longer had any disgrace.

@_ParisBaybee - I Don't Live in Chicago

by **Shawnee Brown, Grade 11**

FROM

Catching Feelings, Winter 2012

Girl (short, light-skinned best friend who I talk to about everything), life on the outside got me going crazy on the inside. You heard about the boy who got shot coming out of his home. That's why I don't like Chicago. I want to live in peace. But how can I when I want to go outside and "BAM BAM I have no tomorrow?" Scars are open. Bars are closing, and I'm still bleeding from the time I thought I was gonna be the one chosen. You know we say we want to change the world; hell, some of us just want to be little boys and girls. We don't want to grow up and be another cur in the world or somewhere slumped over, drunk. Hey, I want to make it. Not another damn statistic can stop me from living out my dream. That's why I don't like Chicago. Drugs killing me; I can't turn around to say, Yeah, I'm gonna live happy. It's too much drama. Still wondering how that happened.

The Magical Adventure: In the Land of Cheeserocks

A Choose-Your-Own-Adventure Story

Continued from page 185

If the zombie was lying, and Uncle Bubba didn't know that the bell actually made more zombies appear, which Uncle Bubba would now have to escape from...

To his dismay, when Uncle Bubba rung the bell, 50 more zombies appeared all around him. "HA HA!" the zombies laughed. The zombie had lied. "We tricked you!"

Uncle Bubba was trapped.

He grabbed a chair and swung it in one of the zombie's faces. But that didn't do anything helpful, it just made all the zombies angrier at him.

How was he supposed to know that chairs provoked zombies?!?!?! He immediately started fighting until the unimaginable happened.

He was scratched by one of the zombies and now HE too was a zombie!

"AHHH!" Zombie Bubba screamed in a new, scratchy, deep voice that sounded like he was vomiting.

He had become green and his hair—well, he didn't have any hair any more!

Then he started to feel dizzy and vomited. Then everything was blurry. He started to feel cold and, before he knew it, he was unconscious. When Uncle Bubba woke up, he was back in his bathroom where he had been transported to Cheeserocks.

But this wasn't Earth. Everything was black and white. When Uncle Bubba looked in the mirror, he wasn't there. He put his hand on his head, but it just went right through.

Was he even alive? He went right through the door and down the stairs. His wife and kids were there. And then he saw a man. He looked like him. But then he realized, IT WAS HIM. Uncle Bubba let out a huge shriek. Everyone looked around. The real Uncle Bubba was dead! He rushed back into the bathroom and jumped out of the window. But there was no portal!

He repeated this several times until the portal appeared and he went back to Cheeserocks.

When he arrived, he saw a key. "This must be the key to free Mr. Frank!" Uncle Bubba thought. Without hesitation, Uncle Bubba rushed to Mr. Frank's house. Maybe if he freed Mr. Frank he could go back to his normal life and not be dead. He rushed to Mr. Frank's house and, yes, Mr. Frank was still in the plexiglass box screaming for help.

Uncle Bubba had not realized he was a zombie still and Mr. Frank would not come out when Uncle Bubba tried to free him. "It's really me! Uncle Bubba! I've been turned into a zombie!" Uncle Bubba must have done some excellent persuading, because Mr. Frank agreed to follow.

"Mr. Frank, you're really not that evil." Uncle Bubba was very excited.

"You too," Mr. Frank said happily.

"Well, I wasn't really..." Before Uncle Bubba could finish his sentence, Uncle Bubba and Mr. Frank were unconscious.

Uncle Bubba was in front of his house. He was so excited that, without thinking, he ran into his door. But he just went right through. He repeated this several times, but he just kept going right through. He was now a ghost. Forever.

Ending by Cole Harris, Grade 3

———

Then, Uncle Bubba went back to Mr. Frank's house and went to the troll. He asked the troll if he could be king. The troll said yes, but first Uncle Bubba had to answer ten riddles. He answered them all correctly and became king. When Uncle Bubba became King Bubba, he made cheese rivers flow. He got along with Mr. Frank, who was the only other person on the planet besides him. So he asked Mr. Frank if they could be friends.

Ending by Sophia Srivastava, Grade 2

———

In Cheeserocks, Uncle Bubba bought a car and a house to live there because he loved cheese. So he ate all of Cheeserocks. He ate soooooooo much.

Ending by Steve Tapia, Grade 2

Dark to Light

by **Imogen Scheller, Grade 4**

FROM

Elementary School Writing Camp, Summer 2012

dark,

scary, beautiful

depressing, concerning, exciting

sunny, moon, dream, quiet

expressing, explaining, finding

funny, bright

light

My Imaginary Friend Is a Jerk

by Amelia Curry, Grade 8

FROM

*Today, Something Different Happened: How to Write Characters,
Spring 2013*

Beep! Beep! Beep!

I slide my hand out from under my comforter and turn off the alarm clock. I groggily climb out of bed, pull on my school uniform, and traipse into the bathroom. I brush out my brown, shoulder-length hair, wincing when the brush catches on a knot.

"You've got a zit," says a girl with spiky, hot pink hair standing next to me.

"Leave me alone, Mariko," I half moan, pulling a tube of zit cream from the medicine cabinet.

"You should really wear contacts. Those glasses make you look like a dork."

"Haven't I told you my mom won't let me?"

The rest of the morning continues on in a similar fashion. Me doing something, Mariko criticizing it. I tread into school, Mariko drifting behind me. School isn't too bad. During classes I can focus on work and ignore everyone else. The problem comes at lunch, that dreaded period in the middle of the day. I hate deciding where to sit. I never know if they were just talking about me or if I'm some kind of inside joke they have. I usually sit alone, but I can't seem to find an empty table today. I nervously scan the room, attempting to find the least intimidating table.

"Don't sit there! They think you're insane," Mariko drawls lazily.

"Mariko, for once in your life, shut up!" Dammit. I said that out loud, didn't I? The thing is, Mariko isn't my friend or my sister. She's a figment of my imagination. Now people will stare. I hate it when people stare. I turn a violent shade of red as twenty pairs of eyes close in on me. Mariko is lucky. No one can stare at her. I should move. I can't stand here forever, or more people will stare.

"H-hey, do you mind if I sit here?"

"Nice stuttering, Kagami." It takes a certain amount of will-power to refrain from replying to Mariko. She's smirking, and I feel myself go from magenta to crimson.

"Sure! Take a seat!" says a girl with her hair in buns, smiling and scooting over to make room for me to pull up a chair.

It looks like many of the other girls are stifling groans. There is a few moments' pause before a forced conversation is started.

"So, what have you been up to lately Daichi?"

"Oh, nothing much. You?"

"Ah, the usual..." The conversation dwindles and stops, and an extremely painful awkward silence ensues.

"Well you've ruined the mood, haven't you, Kagami?" Mariko says in her annoying sing-song manner. Lunch continues on like that. Mariko hurls a few more insults at me, and I barely keep my mouth shut. I'm almost home free as I hurry out of the school at the much-anticipated sound of the bell. That's when I feel a sharp push from behind, and a few seconds later I'm sprawled facedown on the linoleum tile floor.

"Oh, Kagami! I think your imaginary friend pushed you!"

I push myself up to see a tall, black-haired girl wearing a look of mock surprise. I gather my stuff off the floor and hear a chorus of laughter erupt behind me. I want to vanish here and now as I choke down a sob. I don't turn around as I leave the building as quickly as I can without actually running. By the time I leave the building, tears are flowing down my cheeks. How can people be such jerks?

"I can't believe they accused me of pushing you!" Mariko is angry, and her arms are crossed as she angrily floats past me.

"You may as well have."

"What? It's not my fault you're such a loser!"

"Why are you such a jerk, Mariko?! You haven't always been so mean. Remember? When we were little we would have tea parties and play with stuffed animals. You were actually nice."

"When I was like that I dressed like a loser...with that frilly pink dress and long, curly, bubblegum pink hair."

"Like you aren't dressed like a loser now! Your outfits look like something a bad punk band would wear."

"I wish I could just leave! Why do I have to stick around you?"

"THEN LEAVE ALREADY!" I'm shouting now.

"I can't! You won't let me!"

"Then how do I get rid of you?!"

"YOU CAN'T!"

I slam my bedroom door hard behind me and fall face-first into my bed. I want to scream, to smash something. I feel like I'm imploding. I just want to melt into my blanket and stop existing. I roll over to see Mariko floating just above the end of my bed, tears streaking her face.

"I'm tired. I want it to end." Mariko is flickering in and out of focus. I remember the last time that happened. I was eight, and I'd just had a fight with my best friend. Mariko was telling me that I was growing up and that she was leaving. I broke down and refused to let her leave. I couldn't lose another friend. After that she became sour and mean and started looking like this.

"Mariko, how can I help?"

"You can't! You won't let go!" Her hair is turning silver and her skin is turning white. Her clothing blends together until it is a long grey dress. She looks like a ghost. "Why can't I leave? Why won't you let go?"

"I can't! I don't remember!" I'm crying. Mariko looks like she's in so much pain. I search my head, trying to find a way to let her go. A memory comes back to me.

"It's okay Kagami! Time to let go! It's okay. I'm not r-"

"No! You're real to me; that's all that matters!"

"Please, just admit it. It's time to let go."

I remember. It makes sense.

"Mariko."

"Yes?"

"You're not real."

And with that she smiles, kisses my forehead, and fades away.

The Magical Adventure: In the Land of Cheeserocks

A Choose-Your-Own-Adventure Story

Continued from page 77

If Uncle Bubba decides to try to find the magic key...

He looks in the kitchen cupboards, and while feeling in a high cupboard he accidentally pushes a button that opened a secret door.

Behind that door, Uncle Bubba finds the magic key, guarded by a troll. The troll asks Uncle Bubba a riddle. "What bow cannot be tied?"

Uncle Bubba struggles for a minute, but then is able to answer the troll. But the troll won't let him get the key until he answers a second riddle: "What instrument doesn't require hands or a mouth to play?"

Bubba thinks for a minute and then exclaims, "Your voice!" And the troll let Uncle Bubba by to get the magic key and recipe.

Bubba ran to the cage and freed Mr. Frank. He used the magic recipe to control the zombies, and he was able to escape from the house. Uncle Bubba runs to a cheese mountain to get another piece of magic cheese. He carves a piece, eats it, and is transported home.

The End

The Smell of Grandma's House

by **The Students**

IN

826CHI's Middle School Writing Workshop, Summer 2012

1. Stew, violet candy, warmth, corn, pudding. Grandma's house smells like baked, meat stews and violets.

2. Grandma's house smells like perfume, cookies, and noodles.

3. My grandma's house smells like old teeth.

4. My grandma's house smells of nothing filled with sorrow just an empty home never seen never done if so once was now is gone a house of nothing but gone and an empty field of memory.

The Magical Adventure: In the Land of Cheeserocks

A Choose-Your-Own-Adventure Story

Continued from page 77

If Uncle Bubba tried to escape the creepy old house by going through the Zombies' obstacle course to the exit...

Uncle Bubba was mad because he'd been tricked to come into the house full of zombies, and wanted to escape and leave Mr. Frank there.

On his way to the exit, there were three ways to go, and there were no sounds. Uncle Bubba chose the path on the left, not knowing that the center path was the correct one. There was a huge rock above him, and a wall in front of him with a tiny opening at the top. In the hole of the tiny opening, about one millimeter big, was a huge block of cheese.

Uncle Bubba did not know that the zombies were suddenly creeping out from behind the corner, after their night's sleep. They crept along the house, and took a big bite of the cheese. Little did they know they were helping Uncle Bubba!

Uncle Bubba watched the cheese get eaten, and wondered to himself, "Hey! Where'd the cheese go?" Then he saw a zombie hand, and pulled it and pulled the zombie down, screaming, "Where's the exit?!"

The zombie told Uncle Bubba that there was a bell that would make the zombies go back to sleep. The zombie was a little zombie and was a little afraid.

*If Uncle Bubba believed the zombie, who was telling the truth, and goes to find the bell knowing that it will make the zombies fall asleep and he can escape back into Cheeserocks, turn to **page 84**.*

*If the zombie was lying, and Uncle Bubba didn't know that the bell actually made more zombies appear, which Uncle Bubba would now have to escape from, turn to **page 173**.*

That's What Kills Them

by Sarah Meyer, Grade 12

FROM

As the Door Gradually Opened, Summer 2013

I remember standing in the veggie aisle

The air was crisp like the lettuce heads
The carrots drooped half-heartedly on their shelves

While glancing at the rutabagas,
their waxy skin reflecting a fluorescent light,
I noticed the oddly lumped one toward the back

I picked it up

Dented and deformed
its open sores held new life

And I turned to you and I said

"Wow, I wonder how they let it get like this."
Then you said
"Wow, I wonder how you could even pick that up."

And that was that

We teetered and tottered and
crashed the cart to the cashier line
while a rutabaga was left to die with the carrots.

I remember standing in a flowery room—
wallpaper, carpet, tall vases that housed
assortments of lilies and gladioli

Big and blooming they peered at me
as I stood in a long room that smelled like baby powder

No one said anything about the wilting lilies,
fading and sunken
and pushed half-heartedly toward the back

Instead, we stood in that silence
The quietest of us sat at the center

His face pale, possibly smeared with powder,
his box, stained with wooden veneer
Metal knobs sat rigidly on the side panels
The flowers were the easiest to look at
as I listened to stories about him that I could no longer tell you

We left that night with smiles
and heavy hearts
We left hugs and promises behind,
but once we got in the car
we were already talking about other things

The nearest taco place we could stop at,
the business-related things that had to be done tomorrow,
how crazy that lady at the bus stop appeared,
with some bickering spliced into the night.

I remember some weeks later,
standing in my room
I was cleaning out my purse when I found a life and remembrance
card

It smelled like baby powder

I put it on my nightstand and I left it to die with the carrots

With the promises we'll break because we always do
we always
always do

That card practically melted into my nightstand
alongside the heap of things I seem to deem
more important

And I could only wonder how we ever let it get like this.

Six Ways of Looking at Me

by Alicia Faulisi, Grade 11

FROM

As the Door Gradually Opened, Summer 2013

1
On a cold Valentine's Day
to a mother who would leave her behind
a baby girl with a head of thick wild curls was born.

2
Light brown almond eyes that she wished were bigger
a curveless top lip that differed from her favorite celebrities
crazy curly hair she'd never know what to do with
it would take her a long time to accept how she looks.

3
Two hippies with long dreads
were newly married

they worked hard and had fun
but then they adopted the little girl
and gave up all their fun, to work even harder.

4

A magnetic child
people were drawn to her contagious laugh
and crooked coy smile
she longed for their closeness
hoping to fill the lonely emptiness she felt inside.

5

She was constantly in trouble
starting fights with her dad
disappointing her little sister
and cheating in school
but hey
at least it was attention.

6

After her first two years of high school
she realized she had to change her ways
so she worked, not so much on school work
but in her therapy
and instead of self-destructing
she wrote.

An Excerpt From Four Regrets

by **JJ Shankar, Grade 8**

—————— FROM ——————

Poetry Bump!, Summer 2013

I deeply regret whacking a policeman with a candlestick,

But you can't hold me accountable for it.

That wasn't me.

That was Roy, the character I created to let out my anger.

Afraid to Fear

by **Candice Jones**

FROM

It's Not a Book if it's Empty, Spring 2012

Sometimes I'm ashamed to be afraid.
Fearing what's on the outside,
yet even more afraid of the enemy.
I wonder why I always hide the inner
me.
I believe god will protect me,
but how will he know when I'm in
danger?
I'm afraid to show people my true color because
what if people don't accept me?
I'm so busy worrying about fitting in
that I forget who I actually am.
I pray to god that there will be a time
when I accept the fact that I am me.

Six-Word Memoir

by **Darius Watt, Grade 9**

FROM

It's Not a Book if it's Empty, Spring 2012

Love is the best thing alive.

About 826CHI

826CHI is one of eight chapters of 826 National, a nonprofit tutoring, writing, and publishing organization with locations in eight cities across the country. 826 Valencia, the flagship center in San Francisco, was founded by writer/editor Dave Eggers and educator Nínive Calegari in 2002.

826CHI opened its doors to Chicago students in October of 2005, joining 826 Valencia, 826LA, 826NYC, 826 Seattle, and 826michigan. Since then, 826 Boston and 826DC have also joined our national network of 826 chapters.

—— OUR PROGRAMS ——

826CHI's free programs reach students at every opportunity— in school, after school, in the evenings, and on weekends.

After-School Tutoring and Writing

826CHI's site is packed four afternoons a week with students who come in for free one-on-one tutoring after school. We serve students of all skill levels and interests, most of whom live or go to school within walking distance of our writing center. Literacy is stressed through daily reading and writing, and monthly chapbook projects, where students' writing around a particular theme is compiled into small books and shared at family and community readings.

Field Trips

We want to help teachers get their students excited about writing while also helping students better express their ideas. 826CHI invites teachers to bring their students to our site for high-energy field trips during the school day. Teachers may choose from several field trip formats depending on their interests and grade level. A group of tutors is also on hand during every field trip, whether we are helping to generate new material or revise already written work. The field trip program is so popular that our schedule is consistently filled almost a year in advance.

In-Schools

At a teacher's behest, we will send tutors into classrooms around the city to provide one-on-one assistance to students as they tackle various projects—Young Authors books, research papers, journalism projects, literary magazines, basic writing assignments, and college entrance essays.

Workshops

826CHI offers free workshops that provide in-depth writing instruction in a variety of areas that schools often cannot include in their curriculum, such as college entrance essay writing, bookmaking, journalism, comic book making, playwriting, and songwriting. These innovative workshops allow students to hone and advance their skills while having fun and developing a greater sense of joy in writing. All workshops are project-based and taught by experienced, accomplished professionals and volunteers. Connecting Chicago students with these creative and generous mentors allows students to dream and achieve on a grand scale.

Student Publishing

At 826CHI, we know the quality of student work is greatly enhanced when it is shared with an authentic audience. All of our activities are project-based, whether they result in an end-of-project book, a class performance, a gallery exhibition, a short film, or an exceptionally rockin' CD. As a writing center, we are especially committed to publishing student work for students to share with their friends, family, the public at large, and the entire universe. Student publications may take the form of small chapbooks that we bind in-house or in professionally published volumes, such as this.

The Boring Store

826CHI shares its space with The Boring Store, Chicago's only undercover secret agent supply store. The Boring Store offers spy supplies in a highly-secretive way. We have grappling hooks, envelope x-ray spray, and an ever-expanding array of fake moustaches. Proceeds from The Boring Store go directly toward supporting 826CHI's programs for Chicago students.

Please visit us online at **www.826chi.org** to learn more about our programs and to find out how you can get involved.

Barry Benson, *Executive Director*
Kendra Curry-Khanna, *Deputy Director*
Zach Duffy, *Director of Education*
Tammy Fickel, *Grants Manager*
Anna Gross, *Boring Store Assistant Agent*
Abi Humber, *Communications and Outreach Coordinator*
Sarah Kokernot, *Program Coordinator*
Hayley Miller, *Events and Outreach Coordinator*
Molly Walsh, *Boring Store Head Agent*

About
Big Shoulders Books

This book was produced in partnership with Big Shoulder Books, DePaul University's community press. Publishing instructors and students supported the production of this book from start to finish, helping with theme development, editing, and promotions.

Big Shoulders Books aims to produce books that engage intimately with the Chicago community and, in the process, give graduate students in DePaul University's Master of Arts in Writing and Publishing program hands-on, practical experience in book publishing. The goal of Big Shoulders Books is to disseminate, free of charge, quality anthologies of writing by and about Chicagoans whose voices might not otherwise be shared. Big Shoulders Books hopes to make small but meaningful contributions to discussions of injustice and inequality in Chicago, as well as to celebrate the tremendous resilience and creativity found in all areas of the city. This is Big Shoulders Books second annual publication.

More information on Big Shoulders Books can be found on their website at **www.bigshouldersbooks.com**

Acknowledgements

A lot of people have asked us why we chose an atlas to unify this year's Compendium. In previous volumes we let the work speak for itself, letting the reader choose their own adventures within the books' pages. In choosing a theme for our fourth installment, we decided to curate that experience a little. Our book spans journeys in outer space, foreign countries (made-up or otherwise), the future, the past, our great city and our strange brains. The atlas emphasises setting, yes, but it also embodies what 826CHI is for every person—volunteer, student, etc.— who walks through our door. It's about exploring. It's about not being afraid to put yourself and your story out there. It's about finding your place.

A giant part of our programming was led or assisted by a small army of interns over the last two years. Lauren Gill, Laura Mittelstaedt, Billie Pritzker, Francisco Tirado, Shannon Wilson,

Bridget Anne Greenfield, Danielle Littman, Daniel Wonk, Nora Wynn, Vineeth Hemavathi, Alex Lubben, Katy Steele, Abigail Howard, Andrea Ayers, Hanna Ahn, Alison Lacey, Nico Dregni, Jenna Hindi, Lainie Fromby, Alissa Walkner, Becky Baumann, Michael Light, Galen Beebe, Claire Gaddis, Katy Heubel, Warren Yates, Nell Klugman, Ashley Keyser, Nick Saigh, Josh Lesser, Sian Kresse, Daniel Rivera, Bryce Parsons-Twesten, Abby Ryder-Huth, Meghan Hickey, Angela Zhang, Sarah Hansen, Danya Sherbini, Elizabeth Gaughan, Noboru Bitoy, Rebecca Stoner, Mo Kinsinger, Brianna Gielow, Ethan Kenvarg, Peter Jensen, Thomas Boyle, Phoebe Jordan-Reilly, Hannah Callas, Quinn Korreck, Carly Hubbard, Peter Benassi, Sarah Hersey, Emily Beaufort, Roci Pacheco, Elif Karatas, Sophie Lyons, Marybeth Beitzel, Majken Schmidt Sogaard, and Ali Cnockaert—all of work you've done has been invaluable to this book and these stories. Thank you for your work teaching, editing, reading, typing and generally being stellar people.

For their incredible help in this year's *Compendium* review process over several days of reading, I give my heartfelt thanks 826CHI volunteers Taylor Alcantar, Heather Bond, Jordan Brown, Jeni Crone, Sarah Erwin, Elizabeth Gaughan, Carly Hubbard, Josh Lesser, Jane Merrill, Shannon Monson, Danny Resner, and Danielle Santos.

I would also like to thank Emily Beaufort, Amanda Furey, Anna Gross, Sophie Lyons and Molly Walsh for lending their expert copyediting skills to these beautiful stories.

In forging new ways to present our students' best work, 826CHI utilized partnerships with some of the best people and organisations I have had the pleasure and privilege to work with. Thank you College of Liberal Arts Charles Dean Suchar, English Department Chair Lucy Rinehart, DePaul's Writing and Publishing Graduate Program Director Michele Morano, Acting Director Ted Anton, Professors David Welch, Miles Harvey, Chris Green, and Jonathan Messinger for your patience and deep devotion to making the best version of this book. What I would do without our constant emails I will never know.

I would also like to thank DePaul's Jennifer Wright and Mary Devona for their professional services.

To all of the DePaul Master of Arts in Writing and Publishing program graduate students who helped read the stories and come up with concept ideas for the book: it wouldn't be as beautiful of a publication without you. You guys did such an amazing job brainstorming and helping us to create the world within these pages.

In terms of the sheer beauty of this book, our designer and 826CHI volunteer Alison Kuczwara and illustrator Marnie Galloway are two of the most talented artists and independent businesswomen I have had the pleasure to work with. You both captured the creativity and life behind every story so well, weaving it into the very fabric of this book. It's perfect, and so are you.

Speaking of amazing duos, Kendra Curry-Khanna and Zach Duffy are one such pair. Through your guidance and advice, both of you challenged and shaped this experience into one I will hold dear forever. I can't even begin to describe how much I've learned, and it's entirely due to the two of you.

To our printer Marc Moore over at McNaughton and Gunn—thank you so much for your outstanding commitment to the Compendium and 826CHI.

This book is almost entirely made possible by the William and Irene Beck Charitable Trust. To William, Irene, and the rest of the Beck family, thank you so much for your generous support.

Most importantly, my deepest thanks goes to the students who lent their pencils and their voices to this book. I have seen your boundless imagination and gigantic hearts inspire every person who has touched this volume, and am grateful every day to you for sharing them with the world.

Finally, I would like to thank you. Whether you picked up a copy for free or threw some dollars our way via The Boring Store, your experience with this book is the ultimate goal. In reading these stories, you've helped reinforce the extreme importance of young voices, and their ability to change lives. Thank you, reader, for making our little universe a part of yours.

All of my love to every one of you, to the ends of the galaxies and back again. It's been an honor.

- Tara Jayakar
Publications Intern 2013-2014

Our Volunteers

———

The book you're holding in your hands has been made with sweat and graphite and the souls of man and beast alike but, mostly, it has been made by the countless number of individuals who support the worlds of 826CHI students every step of the way. All of our volunteers, whether they helped at a field trip once last June or have been a part of 826CHI for years and years, have had a hand in every single aspect of this book. They are the force behind all of the work we do, and this book wouldn't exist without them.

Michelle Abtahi

Kevin Absil*

Danielle Adams

Abdul-Awwal Adebayo

Marilyn Aguilera*

Julie Ahern

Alejandro Aixala

Taylor Alcantar

Ariel Alexovich

Tanveer Ali

Leah Allen

Sophia Anagnos

Christian Anderson*

Katrina Anderson

Meagan Anderson*

Rebecca Anstee

Melin Arias

Walter Askew

Nicole Azores-Gococo

Theresa Bailey*

Megan Baker

Greg Baldino

Daniel Baranski

Jennalee Battson

Margaret Baumanis

Rebecca Baumann

Nate Baumgart

Galen Beebe

Marybeth Beitzel

Brooke Berbari*

Kalen Berglind	Sarah Campbell	Matthew DeMarco
Stephanie Betts	Angela Campion	Linda Dennison
Mykel Beygel	Debbie Capone	Yaneth Diaz
Matthew Blake	Daniella Caruso*	Tonya Dills
Jodie Bodeker	Meagan Cassidy	Courtney Douglas
Gabriel Boden	Sauravi Chakrabarty	Jim Dudas
Kat Bolton	Angela Champion	Phyllis Dugan
Meredith Boltz*	Ouida Chery	Ashley Duncan
Heather Bond	Rosie Chevalier	Kara Dunn
Tony Bonomo	Kelley Christensen	Amy Dusto
Stephanie Bournakis	Ashwin Chugh	Claire Edlebeck
Ashley Boyd	Daniel Cleland	Nicholas Enquist*
Nora Boydston	Maura Clement	Alicia Enriquez
Sarah Brandon	Alison Cnockaert*	Sarah Erwin
Kenneth Broady*	Michael Cohen	Mychal Estalilla
Nicole Bronnimann	Rachel Hauben Combs*	Kim Evans
Colin Brown	John Conneely	Jourdan Fairchild
Amy Brown	Chris Coons	Brigham Fay
Jordan Brown	Janet Conneely	Claire Feinberg
Brad Brubaker	Katherine Connolly*	Wyatt Fertig
Nicholas Bruno*	Elizabeth Cordes	Jennifer Fett
Adam Burke	Kim Cramer	Chelsea Fiddyment
Linda Butterfield	Daniel Crisp	Ahndria Ford
Amelia Buzzell	Jeni Crone	Alice Foreman
Laura Caffentzis	Bryan Crowe	Colin Foy*
Sarah Cammelot	Avery Cunningham*	Hannah Kristina Fronzak

Heather Frymark*

Amanda Furey*

Claire Gaddis

Alison Gaines

Ali Galante

Maureen "Mo"Gallagher

Bridgit Gallagher

Joey Gallimore

Maria Galvez

Kevin Garvey

Elizabeth Gaughan

Wayne Giacalone

Amy Giacalone

Laura Gienger

Erik Giles

Priscilla Gil*

Lindsay Goetting

Michael Goldberg

Sara Goldstein

Robert Gornik

Melinda Gray*

Kristopher Greene

Katherine Greenleaf

Katie Greenock

Stefanie Greisbach

Elise Hadfield

Theodore Hahn

Caitlin Hamrin

Rajiv Haque

William Harris*

Bethany Hart

Megan Hauser

Nicole Haysler

Michael Hernandez

Gerardo Herrera

Arianna Hess

Maureen Hickey

Hesham Hilmy

Brandon Hinson

David Holtzman

Carly Marie Hubbard

Melissa Huffer

Abi Humber

Andrew Humphries

Katie Itterman

Brenna Ivey

Majda Jakupovic*

Mike Jamoom

Tara Jayakar

Peter Jensen

Abigail Jimenez

Colin Johnson

Julia Johnston

Nicole Johnson*

Jordan Jones

Christopher Jones

Jordan Jones

John Kaderbek

Merrideth Kalil

Basim Kamal

Daniele Karmik

Jenny Kauchak

Elaine Kelch

Julian Kendall

Ethan Kenvarg

Keith Kidston

Margaret Kilbride

Stacy Kim

Stephanie Kirwin

Taylor Klassman

Nell Klugman

Dorothy Knight

Martha Koch

Andrew Kondrat

Rebecca Korab

Greta Kovach

Amar Krad

Pamela Kranyak

Bryan Krastins	Allison Levy	Jeremy McKinzie
Julie Krause	Grace Lewis	Victoria McManus
Amy Krzyzek	Diana Lewis	Bronwyn Mead
Chris Kuberski	Eileen Libby	Jane Merrill
Alison Kuczwara	Alex Liddle	Rachel Mickelson
Sheela Kumar	Michael Paul Light	Christopher Miksch
Adam Kunkel	Kari Lindquist	Christina Mitts*
Justine Kuruna	Abigail Lopez	Shannon Monson
Dan Kuruna	Owen Lowery	Alexyss Mujkanovic
Jentes Kuruna	Alex Lubben	Timothy Munroe
Josh Kurlander	Tricia Lunt	Thom Murtagh
Dan Kuruna	Alyssa Lytle	Megan Myscofski
Sean Lachut	Elizabeth Mabrey	Emily Natzel*
Alan Lane	Hisham Madani	Emily Navarro
Sean Langan	Jordan Maier	Lauren Nelson
William Larkin	Daniel Mann	Michael Noga*
Jules Lazar	Gabriel Mannheim	Michelle Nunez
Carmen Le	Jonathan Mannheim	Kerry O'Neil
Kjirstin Leach	Julie Marchiano	Naomi Obahor
Jenny Lee	Daniel Marshall	Jael Olivares*
Ryan Lee	Michael Martin	Ezra Olson
Loren Legorreta	Alyssa Martinez	Jessica Olson*
Danny Lello	Erik Martinez	Mayra Orduno*
John Lendman	Thomas Matysik	Erin Orozco
Maya Lentz	Aaron Maurer	Aaron Orsini
Josh Lesser	Timothy McDermott*	Sion Owen

Rocio Pacheco	Martin Resendiz	Danya Sherbini
Elijah Park	Daniel Resner	Andrew Shih
Bryce Parsons-Twesten	Chris Rife	Shannon Shreibak
Alex Pate	Jonathan Risk	Shadia Shukair
Uday Patil	Daniel Ristau	Danielle Silletti
Charlotte Pattison	Paul Rizzuto	Michael Ben Silva
Erin Paulini	Peter Robins-Brown	Teshika Silver
Julie Pearson	Drew Rodriguez	Kunal Singh
Shauna Peet	Eric Rodriguez	Robin Smith
Cynthia Pelayo	Mario Romanelli	Erin Smith
Laura Perelman	Perry Romanowski	Dana Smith
Ashley Perez*	Joseph Rook	Abigail Smith
Mary Peterson	Alex Rosales	Andrew Smith
Peter Podlipni	Nicole Rosario	Viridiana Solorio
Annie Pontarelli	Joshua Ruddy	Alexander Starace
Sara Portner	Abby Ryder	James Steele
Deb Powell	Mayra Sanchez	Sarah Steimer
Mike Powell	Elaine Sanker	Nicholas Stephens
Boyda Powell	Danielle Santos	Dana Stewart
Laura Puls	Ariane Scholl	Theresa Stewart
Aparna Puppala	Kate Schriner	Anne Marie Sticksel
Kelly Quintanilla	Shondolyn Scott	Sarah Stoehr
Devin Rapson	Nicholas Scully	Leslie Strauss
Jennifer Remedios	Briana Serbus	Alexander Strong
Angie Renfro	Michael Sewall	Matt Sudman
Aaron Renier	Minti Shah	Gabe Sulkes